Between Public and Private

Between Public and Private

The Lost Boundaries of the Self

Joseph Bensman
and
Robert Lilienfeld

THE FREE PRESS
A Division of Macmillan Publishing Co., Inc.
New York

Collier Macmillan Publishers
London

The Free Press
A Division of Macmillan Publishing Co., Inc.
866 Third Avenue, New York, N. Y. 10022

Collier Macmillan Canada, Ltd.

Library of Congress Catalog Card Number: 78-24751

Printed in the United States of America

printing number

1 2 3 4 5 6 7 8 9 10

Library of Congress Cataloging in Publication Data

Bensman, Joseph.
  Between public and private.

  Includes index.
  1. Social role. 2. Individualism. 3. Secrecy
(Psychology) 4. Intimacy (Psychology) 5. Personality
and culture. I. Lilienfeld, Robert, joint author.
II. Title.
HM291.B388 1979   301.11'3   78-24751
ISBN 0-02-902690-3

Contents

Introduction

The phenomena suggested by the terms *public* and *private* embrace much of the entire contents of culture, society, personality, and social character. We usually tend to think of the "public" versus the "private" in economic terms, as in public or private ownership. In political terms "public" means the government, and "private" means the individual. Since the beginning of society, we have used these terms to debate the question: What does the private individual owe to the public as represented by the state, and what are the limits of state intervention into the affairs of the private individual? These issues have, at various levels, never been resolved; they appear at ever new and ever renewed levels of conflict and resolution, changing their terms and salience, in part on the basis of the failure of past resolutions and in part on the basis of emerging political, economic, and technological developments of the society in which the issue is posed.

In this book we will be concerned with the public and the private as *roles,* as expectations we collectively and distributively hold for each other and for ourselves. The public and private in a sense are part of the self, analyzable as such, and in another sense are the very warp and woof of the operation of society. Much of what we call culture is the attempt to portray and define the relationship of each individual to his or her self and to others.* And every operation of the machinery of society affects and alters both the meaning of "public" and "private" and the relation of each sphere to the other.

Both the meaning of the respective spheres and their interrelationship are subject to endless controversy and debate, depending on our notions of the individual, of society, and of culture at any moment in history. Stating the issue in quasibiblical terms (render unto the public what is the public's, and to the private what is the self's) does not resolve it. For we do not know for any length of time what properly is the public's or the self's, for the very definitions of these terms are continuously subject to controversy.

In this book we shall attempt to show in broad outline how both concepts emerged out of older manifestations of the self, the traditional role configurations in ancient and primitive society, and how, once having emerged, public and private roles have been the object of continuous redefinition and conflict, as the operation of society and its institutions has continuously altered the content and interrelationship of the two spheres.

The controversy has been intense. In the 1960s, for instance, it was said that public institutions and public definitions of the self were so alien and repressive, and that the boundaries of the private— i.e., what one could express to others—were so rigid that a whole new set of social relationships were necessary. The demands by public institutions (government, business, churches, universities) were out of phase with the needs of the private self, so much so that an entirely new set of institutions was necessary: communes, perhaps, or some other anarchical expression of social relations. At the same time, the entire conception of what constituted the private, or the socially defined boundaries of the self, placed such a burden upon individuals that they were unable to express themselves to each other or even to themselves. Under attack was the whole notion of the autonomous private individual, who rendered to himself that which was purely his own. Protestantism, especially the Puritan tradition and that of the Victorian age, emphasized that each individual had to be peculiarly responsible to himself and to his God. There was something indecent about revealing those aspects of the self that were either sinful or socially inappropriate. The individual had to conceal from others

*Despite the continual and frequent use of masculine pronouns in this book, women are included in our discussions.

(and often from himself) those aspects of himself that were socially or morally stigmatic. This made individualism and privacy a burden difficult to bear. Demands for new forms of intimacy, sociability, and communalism to overcome the burden of privacy have increasingly been heard, and responses to these demands have begun to alter the basic established definitions of the public and private in Western civilization. The boundaries have altered. We see a new informality in public behavior, in dress and speech, and in moral and sexual codes, which those of us who are traditionalists may decry. And we see, perhaps as the same phenomenon, a demand for intimacy—an assertion of the right and the need to express our most intimate and private selves, if not in public, then in interpersonal relationships. The private is taboo. But we also protest when public agencies coercively invade traditional areas of privacy.

At another level, we value individualism, the right and ability to project ourselves as unique, distinct persons according to styles and modes that we create for ourselves. We dress to express our individual selves, and we have unique interests and modes of self-presentation that make us, we hope, attractive and valuable. This emphasis on a unique individuality presumes that we do not present to others the totality of ourself. If we are unique, we are special, and we do not emphasize our common humanity lest it devalue our individuality. That which we do not emphasize in public presentations and projections is, for us, the private.

Yet when we emphasize the private, the unique, the individual, we usually do so by devaluing the public, the social, and the collective. When we object to burdens of privacy, and to the isolation and alienation that privacy entails, we affirm the social, the intimate, and the communal. We may, however, still object to the repressiveness, impersonality, and isolation that large-scale society seems to entail. But we also recognize that whatever individuals achieve, it is through the operation of society. We know that as biological creatures devoid of culture and cooperation we are not much more than the great apes. Only through the social and collective operation of society do we formulate the ideals, values, beliefs that make us human, and only by social organization do we both articulate our ideals and develop the possibility of realizing them.

Society enables us to express the best of our human potentiality and at the same time is the source of repression and discontent.

We experience much of this discontent at the social level, in terms of social and economic problems and conflict. At personal

levels, we experience the conflict between the public roles we internalize or reject and our needs to act as deeply private individuals who
at some time must necessarily respond to public roles.

The discussion of the public and the private, as we have indicated, is a constant theme in human history. It was present in ancient
Greece, as expressed in the struggle over the obligations of the citizen
to the republic. It was expressed throughout Roman history, particularly with the rise of Christianity. In medieval cities the problem
again reasserted itself as the problem of citizenship: To whom do the
citizens owe allegiance—the city or feudal society? In the Renaissance the ideal of the heroic, artistic individual reasserted itself. The
creative artist had obligations only to himself and his art. And in the
Romantic era the individual asserted his uniqueness not only in art,
his work, but in his particular style of consumption, manners,
speech, and dress. Protestant theory embodied in the Reformation
had earlier offered to many an individualism based on personal
choice and responsibility, and upon a privacy that was not so ebullient as the heroics of the Romantic artist or bohemian.

By the end of the nineteenth century individualists had grown
weary of the burdens of freedom, and they have become increasingly
so into the twentieth century. They seek to "escape from freedom,"
as Eric Fromm has put it; but they have also felt oppressed by the
denial of individualism, by the standardization that mass public
bureaucracies, mass communications, and impersonal markets have
imposed upon them. Surrounded by a host of conflicting evils, they
have run from the arms of one into the arms of another. Each solution to the dilemma has brought with it its own problems. This book
attempts to portray that predicament. It reflects more than a quar-
ter-century of obsession.

George Herbert Mead was the first social psychologist to use the
concept of roles explicitly. In his *Mind, Self, and Society* Mead explained how the emergence of the self was inevitably an ongoing
process of society. Mind, self, and society were merely aspects of
each other. Mead's analysis was timeless and ahistorical, showing how
the mind and self (self-consciousness), were socially derived. Yet that
analysis seemed to contradict another set of theories, which attempted
to demonstrate that self-consciousness emerged historically. Jacob
Burckhardt had shown how self-consciousness had emerged in the
Renaissance as a historical development, just as Max Weber, Karl

Jaspers, and Bruno Snell had shown how self-consciousness had emerged in the axial age of history, in classical Greece, in ancient Judea, and during the rise of Christianity. Georg Simmel, along with Weber, had shown how the city bred individualism and self-consciousness, together with feelings of isolation and alienation that are a product of individualism.

This contradiction between seeing the emergence of the self as a cultural, historical development and seeing it as intrinsic to the very operation of society is the ultimate problem that inspired this book. The immediate problem, however, was somewhat different. Erving Goffman, perhaps America's most original living sociologist, basing much of his work on Mead, explored the concept of social roles in his early work. More fully than any other sociologist, Goffman explored the presentation of self in interpersonal relationships, emphasizing the self-management of one's self-projection to others, and the self-conscious use of props, settings, and techniques of stagecraft. He emphasized role playing as a means of self-enhancement, and as self-defense against self-aggrandizement by others.

We have taken issue with Goffman's ideas. First, we have felt that Goffman took for granted the total institutional structure of society, conceiving of that structure as only the stage setting within which individuals act out interpersonal role behavior. We will argue that the very development of institutional structures—political, economic, cultural, religious, and so on—is not the background but the basic medium through which both public and private roles are formulated.

Moreover, we will argue that Goffman's motivation scheme of self-enhancement and self-defense in personal relations is far too narrow a conception for human motivation. Religious values, economic ethics, political ideologies, and a whole host of internalized social motives may be as important as the narrowly defined values of ego defense and enhancement. Our continuous interest in, and response to, Goffman's work has kept our interest in this area alive, as has Robert Merton's work, which emphasized, in more positive terms, the meaning of the social component in role behavior. But we have sought to integrate conceptions of social roles with their biological and psychological bases, as these roles have emerged and been redefined throughout history. As a result we have attempted to come to grips with Freudian theories of personality, and at the same time— much more than Freud and most Freudians—we have emphasized the cultural, social, and economic bases of the self.

While we have described the theoretical and academic sources of our interest, we would be wrong to say that these sources caused us to write this book. The conflict in conceptions of the public and private is a perpetual one. We initially experienced this conflict at an intellectual level (we will agree that everyone experiences it at a personal level) through the works of Eric Fromm, Karen Horney, and Harry Stack Sullivan, in the early forties. Such writers as David Riesman, William H. Whyte, and Allen Wheelis, among others, focused upon this issue in the 1950s. Herbert Marcuse, Norman O. Brown, and Paul Goodman were among those who restated it in the 1960s.

In the 1970s, Marshall Berman and Richard Sennett are contributing major efforts to the collective reexamination of the whole concept of the public and the private. This book is our modest contribution to that discussion.

Chapter 1

On Roles and Role Behavior

The concept of social roles, which includes concepts of role playing and of role performance, has been described and analyzed from a
wide variety of perspectives. These include seeing role playing as a
process of social and symbolic interaction, in which the emphasis is
placed on the dynamic process of social action and on the use of
roles as means by which individuals become socialized and express
their social nature.[1]

Roles have also been analyzed as structures of expectancies. A
role—a set of expectancies—is analytically separated from the process
of interaction, and conceived of in terms of its content and form.[2]
Working along these lines, an organization, a group, an institution,
even a society—all can be seen as a patterning of roles, and the task
of analysis is that of understanding how the roles themselves are
related to each other; how they support, maintain, or conflict with
each other. In such studies the focus of analysis is the role, and not
the actor.[3]

Organizations, too, can be seen in terms of the relationships between roles, rewards, values, and the selection of rewards appropriate to conformity with expected role images or role models. Such
analyses are extremely important in organizational and management studies.[4]

On other and perhaps theoretically simpler levels, role concepts have been used in occupational studies to point not only to the processes by which persons become professionals and craftsmen,[5] but also to analyze the meaning and nature of occupations and crafts themselves. Closely allied to such studies are studies of socialization, especially occupational socialization, though of course it is generally understood that the concepts of socialization and of role playing are inextricably interwoven.

In addition to the above, any status attribute at all—age, sex, family, religion, or political and economic status—can be expressed socially through the concept of roles, inasmuch as these socially selected status attributes operate at the level of both personal and institutional interactions by means of socially or organizationally defined role expectancies.[6]

In a more basic sense, the concept of roles and of role playing expresses the means by which the personal life and history of the individual becomes expressed socially in ways that make society possible. Thus, according to George Herbert Mead, while the individual becomes human through his role behavior, society becomes possible through the organization of roles and role behavior.

It is possible to emphasize the public and social and institutional aspects of role behavior, or, alternatively, one can focus on the ways roles are internalized and performed by individuals. The relationship of the individual's total self to a role may be as important as the relationship of the role to the institution. Psychologists, especially Freudian and clinical psychologists, have emphasized the relationship of the individual to the role by use of such concepts as *ego ideal, superego, identification,* and *parent surrogate,* and some psychologists have attempted increasingly to combine the emphasis on roles as expressions of social processes with an emphasis on roles as the means of expressing individual processes.

In this book we will be concerned with the relationships between public and private aspects of the same roles as acted out in situations of varying degrees of intimacy and public formality; and we will be concerned with the differing nature of roles as they occur in different degrees of intimacy and public formality.

The Range of Role Behavior

First of all, one hardly needs proof to assert that almost all social behavior involves some degree of social communication, and that this is expressed in terms of roles, role expectancies, role demands, and so on. Psychosis has been defined as the inability to respond to communications. The psychotic is unable either to recognize role expectancies or to respond to them in ways that make social life possible.[7] At another extreme, it is possible to recognize individuals who respond totally in terms of public or institutional definitions of roles, and whose private selves are almost completely smothered by the roles they occupy. One of the dominant images of modern society is that of the soulless bureaucrat, the complete official, who internalizes his public role to the point of having no other self. The fact that such a person is almost universally regarded with disdain suggests that one of the major role demands made upon officials and other public personages is that they transcend their public roles, or at least let some aspect of their private selves come through. The irony embodied in the notion of socially expected deviancy from social expectancies is compounded by the fact that despite such expected deviancy, the failure of individuals to fulfill their roles fairly and judiciously quite often results in complaints of bias, inappropriate behavior, lack of dignity, and lack of personal control. The basis of these complaints will be discussed later.

An opposite approach that still emphasizes the dominance of the public role, the overwillingness to respond to public communication, is expressed in the application of role theories of the 1950s and 1960s. David Riesman, in his concept of the other-oriented character type, emphasizes the individual who has no inner balance, no gyroscopic center; who, in the absence of a stabilizing core, overresponds to the demands of others. The other-oriented person is so adept at responding to the communications of others that in so doing he reveals the absence of a self—or he is unable to develop one. In the period of the 1950s and 1960s a large literature developed about character types that were "oversocialized." Eric Fromm and C. Wright Mills developed the concept of the personality who so attunes himself to others or to "the market" that nothing is left over for himself.[8]

Much of this criticism of Americans' overconformity to public norms takes its starting point from the criticism of Dale Carnegie's *How to Win Friends and Influence People,* a book which has been an all-time best seller, and from Karl Mannheim's interpretation of the phenomenon that Carnegie represented. Mannheim developed the concept of self-rationalization: the individual's re-creation of himself in order to sell himself in a personality market. The self so created consists of the adoption of a set of social roles that internalize the demands of the relevant publics the person expects to deal with in the course of his career.[9] Mannheim contrasted the self-rationalization implicit in Carnegie's work with that in Ben Franklin's *Autobiography;* Franklin undertook a similar program of self-rationalization, but it was designed to achieve moral perfection according to standards that were originally religious but by Franklin's time had become—or were still becoming—secularized. Franklin assumed that the achievement of moral perfection would result in social and economic success. In that sense, contradictions between public roles and the private self were not apparent to Franklin.

Mannheim's discussion of Franklin, and of the change in the meaning of self-rationalization, was derived from Max Weber, who, in his great work *The Protestant Sects in America,* called attention to the transformation in the social meaning of the Protestant ethic. By the mid-nineteenth century, the evidence of the economic efficacy the Protestant ethic and of sect membership was so apparent that Protestants, eager for the success that had once been evidence of salvation, reversed means and ends. They joined the sects, and tried to maintain good standing in them, in order to have access to markets, capital, and credit. Sect membership was evidence of good standing in a community, and thus came close to guaranteeing credit and a clientele. Weber went on to show that by the last third of the nineteenth century secular service organizations had taken over the function of the Protestant sects in providing the evidence of good social character that assured access to economic opportunities and resources.[10]

The transition from the "inner-oriented" ethical standards of the Puritan to the success-oriented membership standards of sect and service club, using such membership and the social approval it entails as a means of guaranteeing secular success, is a transformation from a social character based on development of an inner self to a new form of social character based on the acceptance of and conformance to public roles that were standardized by sects and clubs. Conformity to public roles thus became a norm for character development in the United States. The literature of the 1950s and 1960s, emphasizing this conformity, reflects Weber's work. William Whyte's *The Organization Man,* following Weber and Joseph Schumpeter, extended Weber's concept to the corporation.[11] The corporation had taken over the task of providing role models for the business and governmental bureaucracies. Conformance to highly organized as well as informally defined public roles had, for Schumpeter, deprived capitalism of its entrepreneurial spirit, and had resulted, for Whyte, in the creation of faceless business bureaucrats called "org-men."

In the 1950s and 1960s a new literature emerged that decried the absence of a self in the contemporary personality. Psychologists and psychiatrists such as Rollo May, Eric Fromm, Allen Wheelis, Viktor Frankl, Kenneth Keniston, and Robert Jay Lifton, among others, indicated that modern patients brought complaints to their doctors that were entirely different from the symptoms of a generation or more earlier. These modern patients complained of a lack of identity, of uncertainty as to who or what they were, of a life that was purposeless and meaningless—of an "existential vacuum," to use Frankl's words. Robert Jay Lifton described modern man as a Proteus—a man able to assume many shapes but no one shape of his own. This modern Protean man was seen as both *undersocialized*—in that, lacking a strong superego, he had no sense of right or wrong—and *oversocialized,* in that he had no self-image different from his social image, and was incapable of creating one.[12]

Weber, in *The Religion of China,* focused attention on the development of the gentlemanly ideal among the Chinese literati, the Mandarin class, under the aegis of Confucian and Mandarin bureaucratic education and officeholding. The Mandarin was provided with a sharply and clearly defined set of public roles appropriate to his public behavior. His education, entry into office, promotion, and official conduct were subject to public review and censorship; indeed his total behavior as a person was evaluated in terms of public role performance and conformance.[13] The Mandarin developed a total character that was conditioned by a response to shame rather than to guilt. Guilt, of course, is based on the sense of violation of self, conditioned by the failure to respond to one's own internalized standards. The shame culture of the Chinese literati was conditioned by a sense of mortification at being exposed in the violation of public standards—that is, of standardized social roles.

Weber argued, in *The Protestant Ethic and the Spirit of Capitalism,* in *The Protestant Sects in America,* and in *The Religion of China,* that a history of belief in the existence of a supra-mundane ethical God in Western society had resulted in the internalization of inner standards of conduct that could be independent of public norms and controls. The individual, in violating these deeply internalized ethical standards, experienced guilt regardless of whether he was publicly exposed in the violation of social norms. Originating under Judaically influenced Christianity, the idea of ethical standards as being guaranteed by an omniscient, omnipotent God meant that a violation of ethical standards was a sin whether or not one was caught in the act. The individual punished himself through his guilt, and was not dependent on externalized public roles and public mechanisms that guaranteed role conformance. The extent to which behavioral standards are promulgated and guaranteed by public institutions, and thus become public social roles, is a central dimension of Weber's work, as seen in his descriptions of such institutions as the sect, the club, the salon, the *cortegiano*, the fraternity, the community and kinship group, the bureaucratic organization, and the church. These are or have been the major definers and enforcers of role conformance. The notion of internally guaranteed personal roles, and a personal sense of one's self, as opposed to a self that is a summation of all one's public roles, in the manner of the Mandarin bureaucrat, represents the opposite extreme to that expressed in the concept of the public persona.[14]

In recent American sociology and social psychology, the concept of public role was largely taken as the norm for studies of socialization. Theodore Newcomb, basing his work largely on that of George Herbert Mead, suggested that as the individual proceeds through his college education he increasingly abandons the standards of his immediate family and begins to take over the attitudes of the peer groups he graduates into. Upperclassman in college provide the standards for the lower classmen; they become *reference groups* for them. A reference group, according to Newcomb and to Robert Merton, who articulated the concept in detail, is a group to which a nonmember would like to belong. He orients his behavior to the standards he imagines that group to possess. The role expectancies he internalizes thus are not of a group he belongs to or of persons he may necessarily interact with. However, he hopes that eventually he will belong. Merton gives the name *anticipatory socialization*[15] to the individual's attempt to internalize a reference group's values.

While the concepts of reference group and *membership group* have added much to the armory of concepts of contemporary social psychology and sociology, they remain within the sphere of emphasis on public and social roles. They deny, at least by exclusion, the importance of deeply internalized personal and private roles, of the private self. This may reflect the sociologist's concern with the social, but it is likely that it reflects the problem of the self, and the problem of the existence of the individuals *qua* individuals. Dennis Wrong, in a brilliant essay, "The Oversocialized Conception of Man," criticized the sociologists of his era, primarily Talcott Parsons, for emphasizing only the social and public side of personality; in doing so, he said, they devalued those motives and activities that a psychologist would regard as basic.[16] The sociologists were charged with ignoring conflict, deviant behavior, and behavior that was not integrated into the ongoing social system. The emphasis on public social roles, Wrong claimed, seemed to leave the individual out of society.

Ralf Dahrendorf, in an equally brilliant essay, "Out of Utopia," emphasized these latter criticisms. Sociologists, he said, in attempting to develop models of a perfect, free-from-conflict social system, confused their theoretical models with social reality, and in doing so, excluded that reality from their purported description of the social world.[17] They thus ignored conflict, as they ignored deviancy except as an unexplained failure of individuals to conform. But Dahrendorf emphasized conflict among organized social and economic units of a larger system, and not the conflict between and within individuals. This of course is not meant as criticism, but it does mean that Dahrendorf did not focus on privacy and the private individual, the task we address ourselves to.

The response to these criticisms of the sociological tradition—and to other criticisms of a sociology that concentrated on the public, official character of the social "system" and its emphasis on cooperation, social motives, and social exchanges—was for sociologists to construct new theories that emphasized deviancy.

Since public and social actions and relations were equated by radical sociologists with the defense of the Establishment, the emphasis on deviancy, especially in the 1960s, developed an antiestablishment tone or rhetoric. In extreme cases, psychosis and insanity in general were defined as the only proper responses to an insane world. For some, the concept of insanity or psychosis did not exist. Such categories were simply the results of labeling by official agents of the Establishment, who used psychiatric social work and sociological labels as devices to isolate and segregate disturbers of that Establishment.[18]

For some, the psychosis that did not exist was produced by the family and by the operation of the insane society. And, finally, a host of sociologists began to describe in detail deviant cultures, and the processes by which individuals entered into and made a career of deviancy. Deviancy could thus be defined as a "moral career" within a culture that was itself deviant from the dominant, "established" culture. The equation of the public, the official, the social with the

Establishment resulted in equating deviancy, delinquency, the psychotic, the psychopathic, and the bizarre with the private. Thus, by a curious process of labeling and definition, the private became the anti-Establishment. These linguistic subtleties had peculiar results. By and large, the private behavior of those individuals whose public behavior was social—that is, it conformed to the vast range of norms that enable an individual to remain out of mental institutions, prisons, and the lower depths of society—was not examined under the category of the private. This is to say that the private behavior of an individual who internalized and accepted these norms without apparent conflict was not examined. At the same time, most of the behavior that was considered deviant, delinquent, exotic, or bizarre was treated as a sociological category, so that deviant behavior within a deviant culture or criminal behavior in a criminal culture was regarded as social behavior, as public and overt behavior. The private, i.e. "normal," behavior of those labelled "deviant" like the private behavior of the so-called "Establishment" types, was not examined. Certainly, the focus of attention of most studies of deviancy in the late 1960s and the early 1970s concentrated on the public behavior of agents of the Establishment: judges, psychiatrists, probation officers, the police, and similar custodial and control officials. Thus, one can conclude that while most "official" sociology of the 1950s and 1960s in principle neglected the totality of the individual with respect to his intimate, private asocial and antisocial behavior, the so-called "correction" neglected, to a large degree, the same behavior.

The neglect of the psychological, of the individual *qua* individual by sociologists can perhaps be understood in terms of the occupational focus of sociology as a profession: That which it studies is more real than the reality itself. Yet sociologists, in dealing with the same kinds of blindness in other fields, would label similar professional narrowness as "trained incompetence" or "occupational psychosis."[19] It will be our contention that the individual is indivisible—that his public and social roles can only be understood in relation to his private, intimate, personal, and psychological existence. This in no way denies what must be regarded as the overwhelming importance of public and social roles. But we would argue that even to understand the dynamics of public and social roles, one must understand their relationship to the self as a totality. Public roles may develop at the expense of the private self. They may, as most sociologists agree, be means by which the private self realizes itself and its potentialities, but tension between public and private roles, it seems to us, must be considered as one of the inescapable facts of life for all individuals in our society, with the exception of either the totally schizophrenic person who lives in total privacy or the automaton who has repressed his private self in order to maintain his public stance.

One of the major assumptions underlying our (and most other writers') treatment of role performance is that the individual possesses a self and a history that is broader and deeper than any one role he plays; that "normal" role performance involves a projection of only part of the self; and that the role performer selects from the total selves that constitute his personal history the responses that are appropriate to a given situation, as defined by his official or role position at a given time and place.[20] Ideally he responds to the role position (status) appropriately, without, however, totally violating the life history—the structure of memories, continuities, and alternative roles—that constitutes his self. While in principle this may appear to be easy, the conflict of alternative role demands, the discontinuities of role behavior,[21] and the necessarily unclear boundaries of role demands in fluid situations make the principle a source of continuous stress, both for the individual and for the organizations and institutions that attempt to organize and pattern certain clusters of roles under their aegis.

The Objectivity of Public Roles

Some roles, especially formally defined public roles, are highly specified and highly structured, both in the communication and organization of expected behavior, skills, and techniques and in the prescribed specifications for fulfilling of the roles. But many public roles allow a relatively wide range of alternative modes for fulfilling the expectancy of a given position. At one extreme, ritual can be conceived of as a series of highly ordered, rigidly prescribed, interlocking set of actions and roles aimed at producing prescribed, overarching psychological states and atmospheres that transcend both the particular demands on any one participant in the ritual[22] and the psychological state induced in the performer. Thus, a religious performance may produce in its audiences a state of awe and wonder, of mystery, exaltation, ecstasy; but the individual performer in any complex ritual must be conscious, must rehearse, must be rational and exact as he counts the steps, the turns, the gestures necessary to produce the sense of awe he induces in others. Through intensive rehearsal the performer may become so familiar with the ritual that its practical application becomes very much a part of his being; he can go through the total mechanics of the ritual without awareness of the rationality that initially governed his rehearsal and planning. At times he thus can share the collective state induced by the ritual. He may be transported, carried away by the awe and mystery he attempts to engender in others, but to the extent that his participation is part of a larger ritual—his role performance of necessity interlocks with the role performance of a multitude of others—he must maintain the precision and coordination of his performance with that of others. His being transported, or "sent," requires a disciplined consciousness that allows him to be precise, accurate, and subject to the overall design of the ritual, regardless of his emotional state.[23] The performer's sharing of a desired emotion with the audience is less important than his contribution to the production of that emotion. If the performer is so transported by the mood he attempts to induce in others that he violates either the mechanics or the measured mood of the ritual, he destroys the intended effect, and may be subject to sanctions based on the inappropriateness of his behavior to the role expectancy demanded of him.

At another extreme, the actor's role behavior may be so rationally calculated, so perfect, that he succeeds in his contribution to an overall effect regardless of whether he shares in the values exalted by the performance. In the latter case, he will be defined as a professional. Thus, the singer of religious music need not be religious; but it would usually be deemed appropriate, as part of his role expectancy, that he not publicly display his lack of religious belief. Such a situation, viewed from the standpoint of the actor, suggests that it is possible for the public role to be conceived of as something totally separate from the inner self, something that is donned and discarded as appropriate to given situations by a role performer who is dispassionate about the content or form of his role behavior but who must acquire the skills necessary to perform the roles. Moreover, the gratifications and sanctions that reward or punish role behavior may be based on values entirely different from those embodied in the public expression of ritual role performance. The singer's primary gratification may be in monetary reward or simply the opportunity to display his skills to an audience.

Regardless of all these considerations, it is important that the individual (1) possess the skills necessary for the public ritual or role performance, and (2) respect the situation, the tone, the mood, that is deemed appropriate for that situation.

Violation of the appropriate public tone, as we have indicated, frequently invites severe sanctions. This means that the individual must master himself to control his moods, his behavior, his public projections, so that the only self apparent in his public role behavior is that embodied in the role expectancy. This focusing of self into role is called "appropriateness of affect," "role discipline," "impulse control," or a "sense of reality." The possession of such self-control is usually esteemed in and of itself, even beyond its exhibition in any particular situation. It is a quality, however, that is not to be taken for granted. Appropriate self-control in ceremonial, public performance is an additional role expectancy.

Role discipline in public rituals may be regarded as a paradigm for many public, formalized performances. Certainly, most of the performing arts impose the same stringent role expectancies as public rituals. Sports, as opposed to play, embody formal sets of rules and highly developed skills, and suggest a public attitude of respect for the rules of the game and for fair play. Many occupations are practiced in public, and this practice requires the use of objective, standard procedures and techniques. Such practice requires the same subordination of self to the role as does ritual. Role discipline is especially insisted upon when the technique is highly developed and standardized, and when the consequence of failure is great. On the other hand, some occupations are necessarily ambiguous in the required form of submission to technical standardization. Virtuosity and skill in the occupation usually require complete mastery of the techniques involved, but such mastery is only a prelude to the ability to work spontaneously with such skills in unstructured or ambiguous situations. In the performing arts, in trial law, in surgery, in sports, the ability to bring an unstructured situation under technical control through personal mastery becomes a requirement for special esteem. Even in these occupations, however, discipline over self in the projection of the expected mood is usually required; that is, the actor must be sufficiently professional not to be rattled or flustered, merely because the situation is outside his control. The courtroom lawyer must be able to counter the brilliant onslaught of his adversary, and the violinist should, according to legend, complete the concerto on three strings with apparent facility and control.

The emphasis on appropriateness of affect and on impulse control and discipline, in order to achieve the projection of a previously defined image and mood, is important in all occupations, professions, and positions that make relatively strong claims for prestige, power, and income. Both the prestige of the profession and personal esteem are conveyed not only by the competence of the performer, but by his projection of an overall mood or state that is designed to bring credit to the performance, the performer, and the agencies the performer represents. Humor is, perhaps, an exception; an underlying principle of humor is that one violates the tone by a manner that destroys a previous, carefully built-up expectancy and quite often reverses it. Humor destroys the expected mood of the previously defined situation, and with it even the image of the competence of the character portrayed by performer, the humorist and often of the humorist himself. The notion of a role conveys a sense of expectations; the violation of the role, its parody, usually after a long, mock-serious buildup, provides the kind of twist that is the heart of humor. But humor exists in special situations that are defined as humorous, as in the telling of a joke, or in revues or performances; the audience expects to be surprised. The same kinds of humor expressed in a situation in which serious role performance is intended may become an illustration of lack of appropriateness of affect, evoking such comments as "What's the matter, you're a comedian or something?" or "You must be joking." Similarly, wit may be the ability to successfully reverse an expected response, often in a situation that is not defined as humorous. But to be witty at a funeral, or in church, or at a patriotic service, is often deemed to be "not funny."

Erving Goffman's concept of role distance—the role performer suggests, by his gestures and demeanor, that he is "above" the role, that the role is too simple or juvenile for him—implies a kind of violation of expected mood. The role performer calls attention to himself by suggesting unexpected ease in mastering a difficult set of demands. His role distance is usually a product of demonstrating ("showing off") his recent mastery of a new set of skills. With habituation to excellence, a taken-for-granted competence usually requires that one project high levels of skill as a normal accompaniment to role performance; such competence is not something that needs affirmation. Thus, a kind of modesty in virtuosity suggests professionalism. Role distance implies either alienation from the role or the recent acquisition of skill; it may characterize a tyro who has not as yet habituated himself to excellence in role performance.[24]

Not only the possession of skills but the creation or maintenance of overall mood and affect are intrinsic parts of successful role
performance. Expertise in mood manipulation must be considered
as part of the role itself, the results of vast efforts to manage personality projection in such a way as is appropriate to particular role
situations. The evocation of deeply inward emotional resources may
require of role performance vast but systematic efforts to induce in
oneself the appropriate mood. It may require fasting, prayer, isolation of the self, attempts to remember situations that in the past
produced anger, grievance, joy, love, or sorrow. Thus when the actor
enters the role situation, he has previously summoned up from his
past the appropriate, expected mood.*

Mastery of the means to give off the desired effect may entail, at
the level of skill, endless pre-performance practice. At the level of
mood, role performance involves training the body, the muscles, the
voice, the emotions, to be available to the will of the performer at
the moment of performance. It means, depending on the role situation, strengthening the arm muscles for handshaking in a reception
line, learning to smile and be gracious for similar occasions, learning
to be tactful and to avoid conflict in situations that involve the
celebration of unity, and learning when the display of anger may
produce the proper note of righteous indignation and when anger is
viewed as evidence of lack of control of one's emotions. It means,
for the role performer, knowing when to appear confident, dynamic,
ebullient, magnetic, and when to be modest, restrained, penitent, and
subdued. And yet, while most of the terms above describe emotions,
the requirements of "appropriateness of affect" mean that these
emotions be rationally calculated and practiced, so that at any one
moment they appear to be spontaneous, easy, unforced, a part of
the overall mood that accompanies the performance.

Such straining for spontaneity may not be as difficult as it seems,
because the variety of emotions considered appropriate to a given
role or position may be limited, and the opportunity to practice is
frequent, given the repetitiveness of most role performances in any
given social position. But real esteem is granted to the performer who
faces a previously undefined situation, in which the appropriate
affect or mood must be guessed or improvised, and who manages on
the spur of the moment to select those gestures and projections that
are afterwards deemed to have been appropriate to the situation.

---

*Of course, as previously noted, part of ceremony may be the attempt by use of music,
chants, and rhythm, to arouse the expected emotion during the course of the ceremony.
When this is the case, unsuccessful role performance is the inability to get into the mood.

In doing so, the performer manages to bring off the desired effect or outcome.

At the linguistic level, this means selection of the words and phrases that convey meanings appropriate to limited occasions, to particular audience characteristics, and to the size of the group. It may involve the selection of words that contribute to a celebratory mood, and the avoidance of words evoking unpleasant realities that would devalue the mood. It may at times suggest that "empty rhetoric," "meaningless phrases," are more meaningful than precise descriptive language that destroys the mood, intensifies divisions within the audience, or causes reflection. On some occasions, lies are more appropriate than truth, though depending on the situation, such lies may be called "white lies."

On other occasions, there must be a discrepancy between the specific manifest message carried in the discussion and that which is subtly presented by the words, uttered by the tone. This is sometimes called diplomacy, at other times, kindness, at still other times, threatening behavior, depending upon the particular relation between latent meaning and manifest expression. The manifest meaning or tone is denied by other meanings or tones that are latent.*

For the speaker as performer, knowledge of how to select and arrange words in such a way that the total effect communicates a message other than that contained in the manifest words themselves, requires considerable skill; and for the listener, the ability to respond to the intended as well as the manifest meaning also requires a vast amount of skill. And for two or more parties to carry on an extended conversation in which no party is taken in by its manifest meaning requires a set of collective skills of a high order; in such situations, one of the indicators of incompetence is the inability to carry on a double or triple level of conversation. To actually say what one means, or bluntly ask other parties what they mean, is to admit the inability to handle the complexities involved. This is judged often as naiveté, foolishness, or simplemindedness. In part, the blurting out of "the truth" is an indication not only of lack of skill, but of lack of self-control. It is an "inappropriate response" to an ambiguous role situation.

---

*"This may hurt me more than it hurts you, but. . . ."; or "I may be forced by circimstances to take a stand that both you and I will regret."

Intimate Roles

The constraints placed upon the actor by highly formal public roles may operate against the expression of less public aspects of the self, as these aspects are revealed in intimate and private situations. We have indicated that to some degree role behavior governs all social actions—that is, socially defined responses to others are a necessary part of all social life. Nevertheless, some roles are deemed more personal, more intimate, more private than others. In general, these intimate or personal roles occur in the peer group, in friendship, in the family, and even in formal organizations when one is not acting in public.

The whole sociological tradition, as well as almost all forms of romanticism—of which that sociological tradition is but a small part—is based on this viewpoint. The basic concepts of primitive society, the *Gemeinschaft*, the small society, the community are based in this tradition, on the importance of intimate, personal, deep emotional social relations and roles. So, too, are the family, the primary group, and the neighborhood.[25] The emergence of modern society is interpreted as causing a fundamental shift in the quality and distribution of social relations. Impersonal roles, whether mediated by money, by symbols, by bureaucratic definition, or by functional relationships have replaced—at least in quantity—the warm communal primary roles that abounded in simpler societies. The newer types of roles are rational, manipulative, segmented, specialized, and instrumental (or "functional"). This shift in quality and distribution of role relationships has been attributed to the rise of the market and of capitalism, industry, bureaucracy, densely populated cities, the mass media, and the large-scale nation-state, and to the decline of the family and of the local community. But despite the objective necessity of these changes the universal value-emphasis has been on the desirability and necessity of these personal, primary roles.

By and large, these more personal, intimate roles are evaluated as being broader, that is, embracing wider ranges of behavior; they are seen as deeper, embodying more warmth, love, anger, and other emotions; they are viewed as more human, and as roles in which one can "be one's self." Thus, they are more adjudged as closely connected to the total personality of the individual.

In their social aspects, these personal roles allow individuals to be more honest and truthful with one another, to express the full range of their emotional attitudes. The roles are viewed as less rational, less manipulative, thus allowing for the emergence of forms of communion based on affectual bonds, rather than those based on limited, rational, narrow, and manipulative forms of association. Intimate and personal relationships have therefore tended to be highly valued. But strangely enough, prestige, esteem, the sense of being sought after, even friendship and love, are often based upon status in highly impersonal agencies such as big business or government, or up on wealth, or celebrity in the mass media. The clustering of such latter roles is more formal and public, but they produce a sense of value for their occupants that make them desirable as friends, peers, romantic partners, and potential spouses. We may decry the loneliness and hypocrisy, the pseudo-*Gemeinschaft* that an official position produces, but we are rarely reluctant to accept such a position. Official position validates our personal sense of self-esteem and gains us personal recognition from others, even when we know that much of that esteem is based not on our personal qualities but on our public positions. Thus, public offices and positions rarely lack candidates, and the competition for such offices (and the roles associated with them) is fierce and avid. Having achieved such positions, we are often able to complain about the impersonality, isolation, inhumanity, and manipulativeness of the roles we are forced to enact. And having failed to achieve (or compete for) such positions, we can lament the manipulativeness and hypocrisy that others practice upon us.

Yet regardless of such complaints, we tend to define ourselves in terms of our private self, and in terms of intimate and personal roles and relationships. In doing so we grant a primacy to these personal roles, even as we flout their standards and seek more profitable bases for our social relationships.

Public and Intimate Roles and the Age Structure

We have indicated that certain kinds of roles are more structured than others, involve less of the total self, require more discipline, control, and self-management, are quite frequently devalued because they do not permit the full expression of the self, but are also valued because they are associated with higher social, economic, and political positions. This latter point requires elaboration.

First, the biological self, the individual at birth, is not initially subject to sharply defined role expectancies. The entire process of socialization consists of learning to respond to ever-changing and ever more exacting role demands, of internalizing these demands, and of learning to differentiate and to shift one's response; these increasingly specified demands become incumbent upon an individual by virtue of changes in age, occupation, organizational membership, and political and social participation.

At a personal level, the problem of responding to continuous new role demands while maintaining continuity with a historic self is critical. The contradiction between the sense of self generated by one's past and the new, unrelated demands of the emerging present is a problem for almost all of us. The normal course of life of almost any individual in modern society requires, both by the process of aging and by the process of personal and social mobility, that the individual continuously enter new role relationships. The partners to these role expectancies may be ever changing, and the content of the role expectancies may be new and different. We have prepared for entry into and mastery of some social positions by education, by "socialization," by "anticipatory social relations"[26]—that is, by self-education and self-manipulation. But in other cases, the rapidity of changes and the contrast between previous and present role relationships is so great that we are not prepared to enter or occupy new role positions. Failure to socialize ourselves to emerging role expectancies may mean that we are not prepared to take advantage of the opportunities that might otherwise be available to us, or in extreme cases, we are not able to "grow up."

We expect, in modern societies, that individuals will develop enough social motility to be able to respond to a variety of new role expectancies, whether or not they have specific indoctrination in, or training for, role performance. But the ability to respond to each and every role demand, regardless of the continuity of the demand with one's prior training and sense of self, is regarded in extreme cases as a form of social psychopathy, or in less extreme cases as an indication of being "other-oriented," i.e., lacking a sense of one's own character. In current social and psychological jargon, this condition may be labelled as "a lack of a sense of identity," or as "alienation." The individual who suffers from such a condition feels that his social responsiveness is a source of problems to himself. Yet the strain of managing multiple role demands while lacking a sense of self—a set of values and preferences that enables the individual to select those role demands he wishes to respond to—may be the source of genuine problems, whether the individual has mastered the vocabulary for expressing his sense of malaise in fashionable language or not.

While all these problems in general, the sequence of roles that become incumbent on a person vary with class, age, occupation, and overall social position.

For all individuals, the role demands placed upon them at relatively young ages tend to be similar.* The initial role demands are intimate. The family, as an agency of socialization, stresses less formal, less segmented, and less public roles. The rewards for compliance with role demands are affectual and diffuse. This does not mean that specific demands for performance by family members are not made, or that role demands are totally undifferentiated. In the same sense, the demands of peer groups at later ages are relatively broad, intimate, unformalized, unsegmented, and rewarded by general patterns of acceptance and affect. But as one proceeds into participation in "secondary" institutions, the individual begins to take on roles that are increasingly public, formal, segmented, objective in definition, and limited in the extent to which they permit the expression of the total personality of the individual. They are also limited in the extent to which the individual faces a set of others who are exposed to his total self; or, to state it differently, as one "ages" one interacts more and more with others in restricted segmented role relationships —others who see, respond to, and reward one for performances that engage only limited aspects of the self.

Public and Intimate Roles and the Class Structure

Given the different nature of these kinds of roles in modern society, each individual in his life history retains and must respond to two continuously different types of role situations: (1) those expressing his intimate personal self, and (2) those expressing particular public, social, segmented selves.

---

*But it is true that different classes may socialize their young differently. Poverty and ignorance may produce nutritional deficiencies; the absence of parents or parental surrogates may produce neglect. In some groups the infant may be treated with great affection at a very young age, only to discover that the affection is withdrawn in a very short time. Some groups and classes may be particularly vulnerable to fads and fashions in child raising, and thus there is relatively little continuity in socialization practices among such groups, especially the middle classes. Upper classes may hire nurses, nannies, tutors, and governesses, permitting the parents to practice benign or not so benign neglect of their children, with the assurance that such neglect is not total neglect.

But the mix of these kinds of role demands differs according to the class and occupational position to which individuals assign themselves or are assigned by the process of mobility, or by ascription.

Those individuals who achieve or are ascribed to "higher" class or occupational roles will find a greater percentage of their total behavior defined by public roles. They become, in the sense outlined above, subject to different kinds of role demands, different from those to which they were habituated in infancy. Those who do not aspire to or do not achieve these higher occupational and class roles dwell in worlds in which the role expectancies are less formal, less objective, less segmented, more "affective," and more diffuse. Thus, one of the major differences between upper and lower classes is in the balance required between public and intimate behavior, and the way that balance is managed. The qualities of being impersonal, of being able to limit and measure the distribution of affect, of successfully protecting oneself from the demands of being or acting as a private person in public, of being in this sense deceitful, are characteristics of the middle and upper classes. Skill in impulse control, which, as we have indicated, means the selective ability to release or withhold the expression of emotion in ways consistent with rational demands, is a personality requirement of the rising middle classes and of the upper classes.

This is only to say that they occupy positions for which the role demands are highly formalized, specialized, and segmented. They deal with clients from whom they are separated by the specialization and hierarchy of their office, and they use the appropriate manners. Preparation for such office entails the acquisition of technical, social, legal, and administrative skills, by virtue of which they separate themselves from their peers and their clients. They are trained to handle the impersonality of office. Industrial workers are often required to exercise routinized impersonal skills such as machine tending, and service workers may do such habitual things as waiting on a customer, but such impersonal skills are relatively simple, repetitive, and one-dimensional. The middle and upper classes will be required to deal with others by means of a variety of social and technical skills. These skills are often more social than are those demanded of an industrial worker. Yet in the midst of such formal sociability, the middle- or upper-class official is required to maintain the distance of his office. He must be amiable, social, or cooperative as necessary— or stern, angry, and distant if appropriate. The social worker, the "boss" and the doctor, the psychiatrist and the priest, as well as the salesman, are trained, or learn, not to overidentify with the client.

Socialization to Public Roles

These kinds of demands are built into the very processes of socialization. Children of the upper and middle classes, and those members of the lower classes who hope to rise, are trained in the ability to respond to and manage public roles. Training includes overcoming the fear of acting in public, restraint on private emotion, the acquisition of "poise," of skills, rituals, "manners," and etiquette. Such training is not only the product of specific, consciously indoctrinated training, but includes, of course, the examples given by parents, friends, and peers, who have either gone through or are in the process of going through similar training. The child will have plenty of opportunity to see his parents treat a stranger in a formal and restricted manner. He may see them manipulate others, or act friendly or angry as related to their rational purposes—even when, as the child knows, they do not feel friendly or angry. The child may witness the parents congratulating themselves on their performance, or this performance may be explained to him. He will also see his parents "let their hair down" among friends—in short, he will see them running the affectual gamut in their role behavior. When the parents act in only a restricted range of roles, the opportunity for internalizing roles outside of that range is limited. Of course, the child may see others—not his parents or parental surrogates—acting out different segments of a total potential emotional range in role behavior, but it may be more difficult to identify with those others. For the individual of the lower classes, whose family and social group do not value the objectivity and formality involved in public roles, the socialization to public roles is not as continuous or progressive, nor is it as demanding. Hence, the gap between public role performance and intimate personal roles is greater, and the fear of entry into public roles is also greater.

In middle-class families, children are under continuous pressure to perform. Such performances include the musical and dance recitals that accompany lessons, and the display of good manners under continuous pressure, especially towards elders and friends of families. In school the middle-class child is encouraged both by parents and teachers to participate in classroom and extracurricular performances at increasing levels of public exposure. At the same time, pressures to attain or maintain academic and extracurricular skills result in a stress on technical competence and mastery of objective techniques and rituals that make for a technically defined distance from others. The lower-class child is usually not subject to such pressures, except perhaps in sports, and excludes himself from the requirement to perform. In most cases, the area of public performance in schools is monopolized by the middle classes. Lack of such training means that when one is "forced" to perform in public, one is likely to do so with awkwardness and to be ill at ease. The awkward performer is likely to receive silent or manifest scorn for his failure and so to be discouraged from making the effort to master the form and content of public performances. His ensuing performances are likely to be done before a peer group, more intimate in nature, and not subject to the criteria of acting before a distant and more impersonal audience.

Perhaps one of the major stumbling blocks in the efforts to increase the social mobility of the "poor" is the psychological and technical difficulty of making the transition from self-management in intimate situations to performance in formal, public situations. As indicated, this is both a technical problem involving training in special skills and a psychological problem involving modes of consciousness and attitudes that make the performance of public roles understandable, desirable, and psychologically accessible.

Individuals and populations not habituated to public roles are likely to see the formality and restrictiveness of the associated role performances as fraudulent and inhuman, because such performances preclude those aspects of emotion, intimacy, and exposure of the larger self that are taken for granted in their environments. On the other hand, individuals in upper classes or in more formal role positions are likely to disdain those who are incapable of handling the narrow, formal, objective roles that govern large parts of their own behavior, and they are likely to be disdainful of the person who "wears his heart on his sleeve."

The ability to deal with formal public roles, then, is a symbol of upper-class status, not only to the upper classes but to the lower classes themselves. When lower classes are able to make the breakthrough to public performances, the achievement of that breakthrough is equated with the achievement of upper-class status, or at least some symbols of such status. Such a breakthrough, when it is made, is often accompanied by a sense of triumph, euphoria, achievement. When this occurs, the ability to perform public, formal, and ceremonial roles becomes separated from the functions such roles usually serve. It evokes a sense of celebration for that achievement per se. It is possible in some segments of societies to find a lower-

class re-creation of public ceremonies, rituals, play, and elaboration
that achieves this secondary effect. The development of the Masonic
order in the eighteenth century—and perhaps even up to the present
—elaborated, symbolized, and burlesqued the upper class, while con-
ferring upon its middle-class members some of the attributes of
upper-class positions. In the same sense, the development of a complex social ritual by the black bourgeoisie, in aping the less ritualistic,
more functional behavior of its white models, celebrates the achievement of minimal status within the upper levels of a lower-status
group. Wherever there is some possibility of group mobility, the elaboration of new yet emulative forms of public roles performance takes
place.[27]

The rising group emulates the public behavior of the group to
whose levels of achievement and performance it aspires, and creates
organizations within which it may enact and mimic that behavior,
but it does so in creative ways. Quite often it burlesques the behavior, converting it into a dramatic ritual, and in so doing makes the
behavior an end in itself, a symbol of arrival. That symbol may be
meaningful only to the aspiring group itself, since the older, established group may not recognize the burlesqued behavior as the
symbol of its own status. It may, on the contrary, disdain it as
evidence of vulgar imitation. Yet if belonging to an emulative group
and participating in its rituals becomes a vehicle of social mobility
by the rising group, a new form of culture is created, and the status
standards of a society become more elaborate. Moreover, the new
culture may with time become transformed, coming closer and closer
to the model it emulates, even as the model inevitably changes. Thus
the new culture may become a bridge to the older culture when initially it was only a parallel or reflection. The new class may enter the
older established class, and the standards of performance as play may
become the standards of performance as work. The shift in the meaning of public performances, and modifications in the nature of such
performances—caused by lack of opportunity to observe the connection between ceremonial behavior and the instrumental functions
served—make the process of emulation more than a process of emulation; for in the alterations caused by imperfect emulation and by the
shift in meanings of the performances in question, new social forms
emerge.

Thus, the ability to perform public roles takes on meanings additional to those involved in the immediate performance itself. The
elements of satire and burlesque involved in the emulation of public

roles may be inevitable in the process of mobility. Discomfort in occupancy of public roles becomes a source of consciousness and creates self-awareness in the mobile individual who becomes an occupant of a public role. The public role, then, is initially psychologically distant to the lower-class aspirant, donned and discarded with a high degree of narcissism, both in the negative sense that the aspirant is estranged from the role and in the positive sense that ability to perform the role is not taken for granted, but is the occasion for self-congratulation.[28] Personal strain, anxiety, self-hatred, may emerge when the demands of objective, impersonal behavior violate internalized self-demands to fulfill roles in total, intimate, personal ways, the latter being a product of earlier socialization to intimate roles. These strains may occur both as an individual "ages" into new positions within his class and as a socially mobile individual substitutes new ways of role performance for his class-bound performances of the past. These strains may also cause inconstancy of performance, such as lapses into personalistic, intimate responses to the demands of objective roles. At times such lapses can be viewed as incompetence (treating public situations as if they were private ones), or malfeasance (the use of personal styles while performing favors to personal friends). At the other extreme, the escape from the ambiguities of shift in role orientation may result in overconformity to specific role demands. In such cases, the individual will repress or cease to display all signs of personal humanity, in his public performance and even in his intimate life, to the point where no intimate life appears to exist.

In his anxiety to master public role demands, the individual may feel that his personal background and habits are a barrier. In order to overcome this barrier, he may choose to repress all personal behavior. He thus makes himself into an automaton capable only of expressing public roles. At one level he appears to be dehumanized. At another level his apparent lack of personal self may result in unintended burlesquing of public roles, inauthentic in its overconformity. Such an individual, while repressing his personal self for the sake of mobility, fails to achieve the desired effect, simply because such overconformity and self-regulation are unnatural to those who have mastered the skills of performing with grace or ease.

The tensions between the different demands of public and intimate roles may be resolved over time, even generations. Thus, secure upper classes are less likely to find the basic contradictions between the two role systems a problem; at the same time, they may find it less difficult to act in the impersonal, segmented manner, and to adopt the objective duplicity of diplomacy and manipulation, required in public roles. But to the extent that the management of public roles is a familiar technique, they are able to transcend mechanical compliance to role demands and act in more arbitrary and personal ways, without the sense of betraying their role requirements or position. They are less likely to be reflective or satirical about the nature of their role relations, since these are not problematical.

As has been said, skill in management of objective, formal public roles becomes an indicator of achieved social status. Hence the skill in management of public roles in their purely social and ceremonial aspects becomes functional in the process of social selection. All upper-class groups articulate and elaborate public ceremonials whose major function is to celebrate their own arrival and position, and in addition to screen would-be occupants of their social position and status. Such ceremonies protect the upper-class members from descent into the lower classes, and differentiate them from members of mobile aspiring classes, because ease in handling of objective public roles and ceremonies clearly demarcates them from those who try too hard and achieve overperfection. Members of old-established upper classes may even sneer at those who emulate them too perfectly.

On a social plane, the elaboration of ceremonial and ritual roles becomes more intensified when an upper class begins to lose its social function, or becomes outstripped by new classes who base themselves on different social functions. Huizinga describes in detail the development of "functionless" pageantry and codes of conduct by the medieval upper classes at precisely those times that the functions ceremonialized are going into disuse because of economic and technical changes.[29] In such cases, the use of public roles becomes functionally autonomous in almost the same sense that the elaboration of ritual in the lower classes is functionally autonomous. The meaning of the public role changes drastically, and becomes, as we have indicated, a creative parody of what once served other, more practical purposes.

Notes

1. The description by George Herbert Mead is the classic starting point. See his *Mind, Self, and Society* (Chicago: University of Chicago Press, 1934), especially sections 20, 21, 22, 25, and 35.

2. Ralph Linton, *The Study of Man* (New York: Appleton-Century-Crofts, 1936), and the section "Status and Role," reprinted in L. Coser and B. Rosenberg, eds., *Sociological Theory, a Book of Readings*, 3rd ed. (New York: Macmillan, 1969), pp. 346-51. See also Linton's *The Cultural Background of Personality* (New York: Appleton-Century-Crofts, 1945).

3. See Linton, "Status and Role," *loc. cit.*, and also Daniel J. Levinson, "Role, Personality, and Social Structure," *Journal of Abnormal and Social Psychology* 58 (1959): 170–180, reprinted in Coser and Rosenberg, *Sociological Theory*, pp. 297–310.

4. Neal Gross, W. S. Mason, and A. W. McEachern, *Explorations in Role Analysis* (New York: Wiley, 1958).

5. Joseph Bensman and Robert Lilienfeld, *Craft and Consciousness—Occupational Technique and the Development of World Images* (New York: Wiley, 1973).

6. Robert Merton expresses the tension between roles in membership groups and in "reference" groups, especially with respect to the U.S. Army of the 1940s. See chapters 8 and 9 of his *Social Theory and Social Structure* (New York: Free Press, 1957). He also emphasizes the conflicts between officials and clients in "status sets"; officials, in dealing with their unorganized clients, have access to professional staffs, secrets, and the resources of other professionals.

7. Norman Cameron, "Reasoning, Regression and Communication in Schizophrenics," *Psychological Monographs* 1, No. 1 (1938): 1-34. See also his "The Functional Psychoses," in J. Hunt, ed., *Personality and the Behavior Disorders* (New York: Ronald Press, 1944), pp. 886–921. See also Morris Schwartz, "A Note on Self-Conception and the Emotionally Disturbed Role," *Sociometry* 29, no. 3 (1966): 300-305.

8. Eric Fromm, *Escape from Freedom* (New York: Holt, Rinehart & Winston, 1941); C. Wright Mills, *White Collar* (New York: Oxford University Press, 1951).

9. Karl Mannheim, "Self-rationalization," in *Man and Society in an Age of Reconstruction*, trans. Edward Shils (1940; reprint, New York: Harcourt, Brace & World, 1966), pp. 56–57. See also Joseph Bensman and Bernard Rosenberg, *Mass, Class, and Bureaucracy* (Englewood Cliffs, N.J.: Prentice-Hall, 1963), pp. 294-98.

10. Hans Gerth and C. Wright Mills, eds. and trans., *From Max Weber*, chapter 12, "The Protestant Sects in America" (New York: Oxford University Press, 1946).

11. William H. Whyte, Jr., *The Organization Man* (New York: Simon & Schuster, 1956).

12. David Riesman (with Nathan Glazer and Reuel Denney), *The Lonely Crowd* (New Haven: Yale University Press, 1950); Rollo May, *Man's Search for Himself* (New York: W. W. Norton & Co., 1953); Allen Wheelis, *The Quest for Identity* (New York: W. W. Norton, 1958); Viktor E. Frankl, *The Will to Meaning* (New York: New American Library, 1969); Viktor E. Frankl, *The Doctor and the Soul* (New York: Knopf, 1955); Kenneth Keniston, *The Uncommitted* (New York:

Basic Books, 1965), Robert Jay Lifton, "Protean Man," *Partisan Review* (winter 1968): 13–27. See also Maurice Stein, Arthur J. Vidich, and David Manning White, eds., *Identity and Anxiety* (New York: Free Press, 1960). Also Joseph Schumpeter, *Capitalism, Socialism, and Democracy,* 3d ed. (1950; reprint, New York: Harper & Row, 1962), especially chapter 28, part 2: "Economic Possibilities in the United States."

13. Max Weber, *The Religion of China,* trans. and ed., Hans H. Gerth (New York: Free Press, 1951), especially chapter 5: "The Literati."

14. See Bensman and Rosenberg, *Mass, Class, and Bureaucracy,* pp. 463 ff., and p. 499: "The Unity of Personality."

15. See Merton, *Social Theory,* chapters 8 and 9; see also Theodore M. Newcomb, *Personality and Social Change* (New York: Dryden Press, 1943), and *Social Psychology* (New York: Dryden Press, 1950).

16. Dennis Wrong, "The Oversocialized Conception of Man in Modern Sociology," in Coser and Rosenberg, *Sociological Theory,* pp. 121–32; also in *American Sociological Review* 26 (1961): 184–193.

17. Ralf Dahrendorf, "Out of Utopia: Toward a Reorientation of Sociological Analysis," in Dahrendorf, *Essays in the Theory of Society* (Stanford, Calif.: Stanford University Press, 1968).

18. Thomas Szasz, *Ideology and Insanity* (Garden City: Anchor Books, 1970) and *The Myth of Mental Illness* (New York: Harper & Row, 1961) are representative works, as are R. D. Laing, *The Divided Self* (London: Tavistock 1961; reprint, Baltimore: Penguin 1965), and Erving Goffman, *Asylums.*

19. Terms attributed to Thorstein Veblen and John Dewey, respectively.

20. See Nicholas Alex and Robert Lejeune, "A Biographical Model: Toward a Microsociology of Memory," December 1977, unpublished manuscript. Also, Hans Gerth and C. Wright Mills, *Character and Social Structure* (New York: Harcourt, Brace & World, 1953); and José Ortega y Gasset, "A Chapter from the History of Ideas—Wilhelm Dilthey and the Idea of Life," in the essay collection *Concord and Liberty* (New York: W. W. Norton, 1946).

21. See Margaret Mead, "Social Change and Cultural Surrogates," in Clyde Kluckhohn and H. Murray, eds., *Personality in Nature, Society, and Culture* (London: Jonathan Cape, 1953).

22. Bensman and Lilienfeld, *Craft and Consciousness,* pp. 18–26.

23. Of course, some orgiastic ritualistic behavior, in which there is no audience, only participants, allows each participant to induce in himself an intensified emotional state of elation, of sexuality, of mimetic aggression, or even grief and despair; but these occasions for which there is no audience represent the collective inducement of purely individual patterns of emotion, aroused in a common occasion. They are organized only in the fact that the occasion is planned and prepared, but the exercise of the detailed activity in a common pattern or design is not prescribed, though an individual who in his own activities does not display the appropriate pattern of grief, euphoria, or transcendence might be viewed as

a hostile outsider by others during and after the event, and might feel guilty for not being able to induce in himself the proper emotional state. Yet because of the lack of an audience and the lack of an organized design to the activities, one might not call such self-induced behavior a ritual. Obviously the borderlines between an organized ritual and an unorganized orgy or pot party cannot be clearly demarcated.

24. Erving Goffman, *The Presentation of Self in Everyday Life*, rev. ed. (Garden City, N.Y.: Doubleday, Anchor Books 1959), especially chapter 6: "The Arts of Impression Management."

25. See Joseph Bensman and Barnard Rosenberg, "The Community" (chapter 5), in *Mass, Class, and Bureaucracy, An Introduction to Society* (New York: Praeger, 1976).

26. Merton, *Social Theory*, pp. 265–68.

27. E. Franklin Frazier, *Black Bourgeoisie* (New York: Free Press, 1957), especially chapter 9.

28. *Ibid.*; also Nancy Mitford, ed., *Noblesse Oblige* (London: Penguin Books, 1959).

29. Jan Huizinga, *The Waning of the Middle Ages* (Garden City, N.Y.: Doubleday, Anchor Books, 1954).

Chapter 2

Privacy as a Social and Historical Phenomenon

Public and intimate roles are social in nature, but each role is based upon a different aspect of sociability. We have indicated some of the strains imposed on individuals occupying public roles. Such roles often conflict with an individual's self-images—images derived from socialization in more intimate roles. But the concept of privacy goes beyond intimacy, for intimacy refers to an individual in close, continuous, and relatively deep association with others over a wide range of behavior. Privacy refers to the individual in relation to himself: his sense of his own uniqueness and apartness, and his sense of having a historical (ontogenetic) continuity that transcends both the intimacy which is in part continuously defined in close association with others and the public performances which exhaust only a portion of his total self. Of course the sense of self, the uniqueness implied in privacy, is in part determined by one's past social relations with others, either at an intimate or a public level. But the sense of being a private individual is something that is abstracted and separate from the total network of social relations that constitute the social basis of a person's existence.

As such, privacy and the value of privacy are something separate from sociability in any of its forms. The sense of privacy, once achieved, is a sense that one is a unique individual, that part of one-self is not surrenderable in social relationships, is not a phenomenon that can be regarded as socially given. It is quite clear that the value and sense of privacy occur in specific historical situations, as in "the axial age" of history,[1] in ancient Greece and Judea, in the Renaissance and in the Reformation. Historically such a sense may decline in given periods and cultures after having been once achieved.

During much of the Middle Ages, in most segments of society, it appears that the social, as defined by tradition and traditional roles, dominated completely the area of personal relations. The individual, caught in a relatively intense social network of a decentralized manorial system, did not—to the best of our knowledge—develop the resources necessary to have a strong, conscious sense of himself. The sense of individuation, the knowledge by the individual that he was a person apart, separate from his society and able to make independent judgments of both himself and his society, began to reemerge only in the Renaissance and during the Reformation.[2] (In the late Roman Empire individualism had flourished at least among the upper classes. Even in the Middle Ages, among the upper strata of the religious orders, individualism, as indicated by high levels of self-consciousness, existed, in part reflecting the concerns of the theologically gifted with their relationship to the universe, as defined in theology.[3]) Even when individuation began to reemerge, it occurred among a relatively small proportion of the total population. The Renaissance was primarily an affair of the artist and an emerging bourgeoisie, who could abstract themselves from traditional social relations, and could assert themselves as individuals against the traditional norms that devalued their uniqueness as individuals. The Reformation, based in part on the ability of individuals to read, i.e., on printing, gave to the literate individual the ability to assert his direct relationship to God, and therefore to assert a more unique subjective experience of religion and interpretation of his world. But even with these changes, the number of people who could assert themselves as individuals was small. The process of individuation, which reemerged in the early Renaissance, has been continuous in its impact on ever larger numbers of individuals in the Western world. An emphasis on individualism, on the social value of privacy, is a historical phenomenon, subject to specific historical, economic, and political causations.

Yet even within a given historical period, the opportunities to achieve a highly developed sense of self, and the social conditions necessary for a sense of privacy, are not equally distributed in a society or population. At a relatively simple level, population density, or perhaps the density of social relationship, can frame the opportunities for privacy. But a person presumably living in a frontier situation, relatively isolated, also has the opportunity, or rather is forced, to exist as a private individual; whether in fact he has the cultural, intellectual, or personal resources to develop the sense of self made possible by his ecological position is problematic. The social isolation of the frontier may result only in brutishness. The individual may respond minimally to nature and the external forces of nature that govern his isolated behavior. Other factors are necessary.[4] Most rural situations in the world today, and through most of our historical past, have not been conducive to the development of the most valued forms of privacy. Two factors might explain this: (1) patterns of rural settlement are such that overcrowding exists in village communes, even though vast acreages of adjoining lands are relatively empty; (2) rural societies in general tend to construct intricate networks of ceremonial and ritual social relations that prevent the achievement of privacy in the psychological meaning of the term. In such isolated social worlds, more often than not, there is a fear of privacy. In primitive societies individuals who draw away from the collective ritual and ceremony, from the overarching networks of social relations, are often thought of as practicing witchcraft, as conspiring against the group, and devaluing the ritual and ceremony, the public life that binds the community together. Even in more sophisticated cultures, the person who appears to withdraw from the public social ritual is conceived of as singular, standoffish, snobbish, or "odd."* He puts distance between himself and the public world, and therefore he appears to be devaluing that world. To the extent that the individual recognizes social participation as a norm, he may find it necessary to overcome his own sense of self, his own private world, in order to avoid censure or the opportunities that might be foregone by censure. The person with a strong sense of private self may consciously attempt to cultivate and fake social participation or the appearance of being social, in order to avoid stigma. Thus, privacy becomes devalued not only by the community but by individuals with a strong sense of self.[5]

In a sense, then, the fear of privacy tends to negate opportunities for privacy in the psychological meaning of the term. Sometimes the

---

*This was clear in the Salem witch trials, and in more sublimated forms it occurs in all cultures where stress is placed on unity.

rejection of privacy is celebrated as and transvalued into the triumph of sociability, mutual self-help, communal values operating in the real world. At the same time, genuine privacy in both rural and urban worlds is often a matter of simple economics. Privacy is achieved by the purchase of space. The ability to shield oneself from the direct observation of others may consist in the ownership of enough land of the right kind. And it includes the wherewithal to own a large enough household and large enough rooms such that one simply has time and space to oneself. Since only the well-to-do can afford ecological privacy, the development of privacy is minimally conditioned by the growth and distribution of wealth.* In the Middle Ages only the upper classes could afford privacy, but the rise of the bourgeoisie in the Renaissance made it accessible to an increasing portion of the population.[6] Even in medieval times it was true that when privacy was highly valued, e.g. for religious reasons, the pious hermit could withdraw into a cave and practice a theologically sanctioned privacy. But such privacy was valued only for the religious virtuoso and was not available to large numbers. In monasteries and priories, privacy could be achieved by self-seclusion in minimally adequate cells, but even this kind of privacy was made possible only by vows of poverty and by public support from those who could not afford or did not desire such privacy for themselves.

Lack of affluence usually means not only large families but over-crowding. As we have indicated, the opportunity to achieve privacy in the ecological sense generally necessitates (1) housing that has sufficient space to allow an individual to spend at least part of his time with himself, and (2) sufficient income to withdraw from economically enforced sociability. This includes in the modern world the ability to finance vacations at the seasonal or weekend retreat and the opportunity through travel to abstract oneself from familiar social relations. Thus, the opportunity to exist as a private individual is governed by affluence. Lower classes are forced to live in situations of intimacy whether or not that intimacy is valued or desired.

---

*The fact that upper classes can afford privacy does not always mean that they will avail themselves of the opportunity. In medieval society the privacy of the dining room and bedroom that middle and upper classes assume today was not available even to manor lords. Retainers, subjects, and servants usually ate and often slept in the same room with the manor lord and his wife. Lack of heating may have been a factor, but more importantly, privacy must be valued before it becomes a social factor in the use of space. Once valued, the use of privacy requires space and the maintenance of distance from others, which most often must be purchased at considerable expense. See Lawrence Stone, *The Family, Sex and Marriage in England, 1500-1800* (New York : Harper & Row, 1977), pp. 253-57.

Individuals in all classes can privatize their behavior either as a result of psychological problems or of their inability to maintain satisfactory social relations. Although internally or externally imposed privacy is independent of class, family resources enable some individuals to endure its burdens more comfortably. This kind of privacy is caused by psychological and social deficiencies and is not an authentic development of a sense of self. It is a privacy imposed upon individuals by weakness, and is always stigmatized. It cannot be conceived of as an enlargement of the self or of the individual's personal resources, but only as a burden under which the individual must suffer. In addition, in urban environments poverty and extreme lower-class status, often indeed outcast status, can impose conditions bordering on privacy. In some societies privacy is related to caste. The outcast is driven into privacy, unless he can share his status with other outcasts. The lower-class person, the tabooed individual, the outcast, must endure the burden of privacy because of avoidance by others. In all of these cases privacy is not an option given to the individual; it is forced upon him. While he cannot enjoy the benefits of sociability, such an individual frequently lacks the resources or the desire to benefit from the possibilities of privacy.

The upper classes can, if they choose, enjoy situations of privacy despite the fact that much of their total life is bounded by both the biological necessity of intimacy and by the necessity or desirability of making public performances. Thus, if we wish to consider the range of role options available for individuals as a result of social class, lower classes focus their social existence in relatively narrow, informal, intimate social relations, as described earlier; upper classes have, as indicated, the necessity and the opportunity for freely given intimate social relations, yet these are less visible or prominent, since a strong proportion of their behavior is governed by formal, objective public roles. And yet the very narrow, segmented nature of their public social roles allows them to withdraw from these roles into enclaves designed for private existence, which at times compensate for the constraints placed upon them by their public and intimate roles. The lower classes do not have these options to alternatively perform public and private roles; they lack both the discretionary power and the resources to do so. Thus mobility in role orientation becomes a social and personal requirement for upper-class individuals. The complexities of handling widely different systems of role management become the immediate problem for upper-class individuals, while the lack of both opportunity and training in this kind of role flexibility becomes the problem for the lower class. The tensions caused by movement from one predominant form of orientation to the other—from rigid intimate role orientations to flexible movement between public and private behavior—become a problem for middle and ascendant classes.

Privacy and the Media

Certainly the possibility of privacy, and its relationship to both public and intimate behavior, are products of the organization and structure of recreation and leisure. In primitive society, as we have indicated, leisure and recreation were public, social conditions associated with public ceremony and ritual, and privacy was either frowned upon or deemed an unusual state associated with witchcraft or with possession by gods or evil spirits. Games, sports, and hunting have always been viewed as public and social occasions, regardless of the formal organization of society. Literacy, by necessity, requires a sense of isolation from the external world in order to concentrate on the book or manuscript being read, and this is true whether the reading is done in public or in private. But reading makes privacy both respectable and tolerable, and so literate classes have always had opportunities to legitimate and express their inclinations for privacy.

The growth of literacy, which accompanied increasing educational opportunities and the rise of the bourgeoisie, made for the possibility of a meaningful privacy. In some societies and segments of society, however, spending too much time reading, as Don Quixote did, is a symbol of withdrawal from public activity, an indication of singularity, eccentricity, or madness; the disapproval of reading becomes a way of expressing disapproval of the privacy that reading objectifies and screens. The discovery and invention of hobbies is a nineteenth-century phenomenon that gave content to the possibility of exploiting opportunities for privacy, and hobbies, too, were undoubtedly pursued predominantly among the middle and upper classes.

The development of the performing arts, which are always associated with either urbanism or the upper classes, made possible the development of public performances; but for the upper-class patron, his attendance *was* a public performance. He, too, was on stage when he observed the actors on stage; the audience observed him as much as they observed the actors.[7] For the lower class in a mass audience, opportunities for privacy could occur amidst the crowd. Thus public performances could, in the anonymity of the crowd, increase the opportunities for freedom from the bounds of intimate behavior while also increasing the opportunities for public performances of actors and patrons.

The boundaries between public and private disappear in the mass media. One of the characteristics of radio and television is the possibility of achieving the illusion of mass participation in the noise they provide, thus achieving some of both the privacy and the public atmosphere of a mass audience when the street scene or mob enters one's living room. At the same time the television set—particularly through the drama, the cinema, and the dance—often projects vivid images of private life. The intimate, the personal, the sexual is publicly celebrated, but strangely enough the sense of privacy is often achieved even in one's home by turning off the television set.

While the mass media increasingly dramatize the inner life of their *personae*—their sexual "problems" and expression, their inner psychological conflicts, their perversions, delusions, and failures— they do so by projecting them in relatively standardized ways. The portrayal of the private is thus objectified by the mass media, though their subject matter is the subjective existence of their protagonists. To the audience, subjective existence takes on a standardized, objective character that nullifies the subjective character of the subject matter. This is especially true when the content of such media presentations is the object of repeated discussion by the audience. The audience, in its discussion, both at a public and a private level, treats the intimate life of the hero or heroine (e.g., Mary Hartmann) as a public issue. In doing so, it is likely that the subject matter per se of the endless private foolishness of Mary Hartmann becomes a public object independent of its relationship to Mary Hartmann. Thus the subject matter which one hundred years ago might have been regarded as taboo for public discussion becomes the ordinary subject matter of ordinary people without specific reference to the content of the mass media. The objectification of subjective private experience has become a major phenomenon of our time.

To be sure, the mass media ought not to be given exclusive credit or blame for such a phenomenon; the "serious" arts, (abetted by the invention of printing) began this process over three centuries ago. Rousseau's *Confessions* may well have been among the first public transvaluations of the private; and the novel, since its first emergence as a genre, has explored virtually all the dimensions of privacy, becoming, however, increasingly explicit in the portrayal of sexuality and the various forms of private perversity, including the psychotic, Certainly, the development of psychology itself—which could not evolve without its subject matter becoming an object of lay, i.e. public, discussion—legitimated public discussion of the private, the intimate, and its objectification. Yet the biography, the novel, even psychological science itself, were initially diffused through the printed word, and meant to be read in private. Nevertheless Freud, whose views were disseminated in print, has been belabored as devaluing the deeply personal, the private, the intimate, the sacred, by making it a topic for public discussion. In adopting a world view as defined by Freud, it is charged, nothing is left sacred; our acceptance of the intimate as a legitimate object for public discussion permits no one to have an area of inner privacy and peace. All personal reserve is abolished, and we increasingly parade our private perversions in public.[8] The pervasiveness of the film, of television, have all tended to make not only their subject matter but the media themselves amenable to the public reception of the private and therefore an additional dimension of objectification.[9]

At some levels this public acceptance of the private has resulted in overcoming the sense of isolation that the very term "privacy" implies; and the recognition that "everyone" suffers by the millions from similar problems, perversities, and "malfunctions" has tended to lighten the load of guilt that an individual may feel if he suffers alone, in private. It may well be true that the load of guilt morally sensitive individuals have perhaps had to carry has been lightened by the mass media. Whether it is desirable to lighten that load is subject to endless discussion, for it can be argued that moral sensitivity and the sense of being a unique individual having moral choices to make is thereby diminished. Thus, the objectification of privacy in the mass media may result in the devaluation of privacy itself.

The Historic Development of Role Orientations

We have indicated that it is possible to conceptualize roles as intimate, public, and private; we have indicated that each type of role places different requirements on the total personality and causes differing orientation problems, and that various role "mixes" are differentially distributed among the population of any given society. Beyond this, we can indicate that the distribution of roles classified as above differs with the development of societies. Primitive society was dominated by a high incidence of public roles; yet the traditional roles were essentially different from the public roles described above. The predominance of ceremony and ritual, the relatively small size of primitive societies, meant that intimate roles and public roles were not sharply differentiated. The small size of such societies meant that everyone lived in public; ceremony and ritual tended to make the collective public life central to the society.

What is more, privacy, as indicated above, was evaluated negatively. To the extent that the primitive society did have a highly articulated stratification system, chiefs and other ceremonial leaders were at the top. Such leaders necessarily occupied roles that were more visible and more public than those of their followers. If there was an initial distinction between public and private roles, it was less a qualitative distinction and more a quantitative one. The chiefs lived only slightly more in public than did their followers. In terms of ceremony, social roles—as we have previously noted—were objective and prescribed. The continuity in socialization prepared individuals for the occupation of these roles. The private individual *qua* individual did not exist to any extent, and his private existence was at most a minimally tolerated fringe behavior expressed by personal peculiarities in the way standardized roles were enacted.

Privacy, however, must have existed in the deviancy necessary to create and construct public ceremonies, since such constructions necessarily involved departure from previous patterns of behavior and creativity, even in societies where conformity to ongoing institutions, and ritual was demanded, as Radin and Malinowski indicate. This is only to say that where change occurs, somebody—an individual—must have initially made the change. The change may have been accepted and adopted by others. but the first act could have been performed only by an individual, whether or not that individual was conscious of the deviancy of his act from public norms. Given the strong tendencies toward traditionalism in primitive societies, one must infer that even minimal changes required unusual amounts of daring and, in terms of the norms of society, strong amounts of individuality.[10]

Opportunities for the development of privacy must have

occurred at times of social disruption (war, famine, migration) and economic and political change, for the prescribed, standard, socially objective roles would have been inadequate for new situations. Yet the relatively slow rate of social change undoubtedly resulted in the continuing predominance of public ritual and ceremonial roles.

The development of privacy as a socially valued trait probably emerged in religion. Primitive charismatic religions and religious movements have often been based on the notion of an extraordinary religious hero—a magician, a prophet, or a military savior—who was able to concentrate in himself the extraordinary powers of the gods, spirits, or *mana* that were believed to characterize the supernatural realm. The process by which the charismatic hero received the grace of a god involved the cultivation of privacy. He isolated himself from his followers or tribe, to mortify and purify himself, to use exotic drugs and chemicals that helped him achieve a private vision. On his return to the community, he announced and objectified that vision, and used it to make demands upon would-be disciples to follow him in religious, military, or political ventures and movements. To the extent that he was able to convince his followers of his possession of supernatural powers, he was treated as a being apart, not subject to ordinary rules, and was able to define himself and the conduct of others. In the midst of his public role, he cultivated and received recognition for a god-given privacy, the right to define his own conduct. Charisma in this sense means an initial retreat from the "objectivity" of established custom into a private, sacred world, during which the charismatic hero uniquely receives a god-given message. He then objectifies and "socializes" that message by demanding compliance from others with his god-given demands.

Other developments in the sphere of religion began to make possible a more "normal," i.e. routinized, private sphere.[11] This occurred with the emergence of notions of a personal God, who directly interacts with isolated individuals. The development of salvation religion devalued the role of extant primitive social ceremony, community-oriented priesthood, and community religion by emphasizing personal religion, this was followed by the professionalization of priesthoods that became concerned with the salvation of the individual rather than the success of the community. This development was undoubtedly the product of the failure of community-oriented religion to provide the gratifications it promised. These gratifications were success in war and the hunt, sufficient rain, good crops, and the success of the community in its collective enterprises, rather than the success of the individual. Religions oriented toward the salvation of the individual attempted to deal with the success and failure of individual efforts, the differential incidence of good and bad fortune, in contradistinction to the success and failure of the community as a totality. An individual could succeed in the midst of community failure and could fail in the midst of general prosperity. Given human mortality, the failure of the individual is ultimately inevitable—if he values life itself—while the community does not necessarily fail in this respect. The new salvation religions ministered to the aspirations and anxieties of individuals in opposition to those religions that served the needs of an entire community. In doing so, they necessarily focused emphasis on the individual and those aspects of his or her life that were not emobdied in social and collective activities. They necessarily emphasized the private existence of the individual, and the sense of apartness involved in that private existence.[12]

Individualism and therefore privacy became a value of ancient Judaism, classical Greece, and early Christianity; but the number of people to whom such values were accessible in such ancient societies was limited. This limitation was maintained by the very nature of ancient and also feudal society. The pyramidal structure of the societies, based on agriculture; the existence of serfdom and slavery; the lack of access to education—all meant that the opportunity to gain the personal resources and culture to cultivate the values that support privacy were not available to the vast bulk of the population. Even in medieval society, privacy and the cultivation of privacy were treasures available to a privileged few. The bulk of the population lived out traditional intimate roles provided by spatially isolated communities. The upper classes to some degree performed public roles with varying degrees of withdrawal into private roles. The breakdown of feudalism, the rise of the Italian city-state, and the emergence of a new bourgeoisie, together with the rediscovery of the values of classical art and literature, resulted—again for a few—in the celebration of individualism, of creativity, of privacy; and with the rise of the bourgeoisie, new and larger classes began to create a new ceremonialism and ritualism in which public roles began to take on, in many respects, a charade-like character.

The development of public roles is ultimately related to both the development of complex systems of stratification and the emergence of the city. Primitive society was organizationally simple; apart from religion, the two dominant institutions were kinship structures and the locality, the community itself. Tribal leaders tended to be heads of powerful families who owned and managed property in the name of the tribe. The development of relatively complex organizations consisted of the expropriation of extended kinship property by tribal chiefs, and the conversion of that property to their own personal property, which was then passed on by inheritance to their immediate lineages.[13] At the same time, but in other places, conquest of one tribe by another resulted in the emergence of new upper classes who expropriated the property of the conquered tribes for their own private and/or tribal use. But in both cases, the processes of stratification and domination that resulted included new kinds of public roles. The new upper classes occupied increasingly segmental public roles that were distinct from the traditional and diffuse community-wide public and ceremonial roles of the past. These new roles were formalized and explicit. To the extent to which the new upper classes were removed from continuous interaction with a community, a part of their life was free from community control. Privacy in the sense of freedom from public scrutiny was part and parcel of the new public roles that were available only to an emerging dominant class or caste. But some of the activities of the new upper classes were performed in public, i.e., became part of their public roles. These included the performance of public rituals and ceremonies, the public conduct of official business, attendance at public functions, and the measured and managed appearance of the official in public audiences, levees, and social affairs. But the political discretion available to power holders allowed them to separate certain aspects of their life from the life of their society.[14]

Even in the sixteenth century, the boundaries between public life and family life were not in any way definite. The family was not closely defined, nor were degrees of distance of descent. The upper-class family lived in public with friends, vassals, and close and distant relatives, and had little opportunity for privacy. Lawrence Stone has called this the open family system.[15]

The growth of cities was far more important than the refinement of stratification systems in the development of both public roles and privacy. In primitive agrarian societies, to repeat, one's personal status was related to position in an extended kinship system. The individual did not exist *qua* individual but only as a member of a family, subject to the role demands incumbent upon him by virtue of the position of his family and his own position in that family. The development of cities and the growth of commerce and wealth associated with cities produced in the ancient and late medieval worlds individuals of power and wealth, especially the latter, who were outside the kinship organization of the tribe or the *polis* (city-state). Since they were outsiders, these new urbanites did not receive the power and prestige that they would have received had they based their claims on family position; they did not enjoy the status of landed agrarian families.[16] Some of the outsiders, even in ancient Greece, agitated for rights and duties that would accrue to them *as individuals,* as citizens, regardless of lineage. Some attempted to elevate the status of their families and thus become part of the dominant political and class system, and others attempted to bring down the traditional system that denied them the rights to which they aspired. Citizenship in a *polis* implied the recognition of the status of an individual (usually one possessing property) and not of a family. But citizenship implied more than this; for as new wealth in commerce and trade, and in the rise of handicraft industries, brought more and more people into the cities, the emerging cities came into existence outside the framework of traditional agrarian society. Citizenship required new roles, and the citizen was expected, as an individual, to perform public duties for the *polis.* The citizen was required to serve in the armed forces of the city; to serve as a legislator, a magistrate, a policeman (as member of the night watch); he was expected to provide in part for the sanitation of the city, its lighting, its fire protection. In fact, he was asked to provide, through his personal effort, all of the municipal services that local civil governments would not provide until the mid-nineteenth century.[17]

Sometimes he provided these services as an individual, or arranged to have a substitute. At other times he provided the services as a member of a merchant or craft guild. The guild was expected to contribute both money and the services of its members to maintain the city. In addition, members became officials of their guilds, and as such were expected to fulfill a new type of public role. Both the role of citizen and the role of guild member tended to be sharply defined, and by virtue of such definition they were separate, narrow roles. When role definition is explicit, separate, or narrow, those aspects of behavior that are not so defined are left to the private existence of the individual. There are, however, exceptions. If the entire system of family, citizenship, and guild roles is so comprehensive and so tightly articulated that no room for individual behavior is left over, then privacy and private roles need not exist. But such a highly developed state of role integration and role supervision is difficult to attain in a complex urban development. In those medieval cities that were small and had powerful guilds, guild roles tended to govern a large part of the public and private life of the individual guild member; but wherever the city grew rapidly and the guilds were not able to absorb the resultant inflow of members, or when guild structures weakened, urban life was characterized by a weak articulation of the role behavior expected by the citizen and by the inability of organizations to enforce conformity to their role expectancies. The failure to produce an overarching "system" of role expectancies that embraces the total life of the individual can called *anomie*.[18] Such *anomie* allows for an individualism based on lack of social or moral order, but it is an individualism nonetheless. But for the most part, the rise of cities in the ancient, medieval, and modern worlds up to the nineteenth century was accompanied by the development of civic roles. The citizen was presented with a clear notion of civic obligations, rights, and privileges, which defined his place in an urban world. These highly articulated public roles, however, being limited, allowed at the same time for the conception of the citizen as a private person. But part of his obligation as a private person consisted of the obligation to develop himself in moral, cultural, and intellectual terms—i.e., to be civilized, and to respect the rights of others who were also expected to be civilized.

These patterns of role formation emerged in ancient Greece and in Judea; they were submerged by the external conquest of Judea and ancient Greece but reemerged contemporaneously in ancient Rome, then in the medieval cities of southern Europe, and in the Renaissance and Reformation periods that followed.

Civic roles were weakened by the massive urbanism of the eighteenth and nineteenth centuries, when peasants who were uprooted from traditional familistic and communal cultures flooded to the cities. Their numbers were so great that civic organizations did not have either the time or the resources to produce the civic socialization that inculcates civic roles. At the same time, changes in the larger society diminished the power of the city to cope with the problems of civic socialization.

Two additional factors are important. First, the rise of the national state resulted in a concept of national citizenship that tended to diminish local civic loyalties. The national state was distant from the individual citizen and dealt with the citizenry as a mass, as a distant category. It was not able to implement its articulation of role expectancies in a direct, personal, and organized manner. The expectances became increasingly symbolic; patriotism, nationalism, and their rhetoric replaced meaningful duties that could be directly imposed upon and voluntarily accepted by the citizenry.

The second factor or perhaps an alternative statement of the same phenomenon, the professionalization of municipal and public services, occurred in the nineteenth century. Those duties that had earlier been demanded of the urban citizen—relating to sanitation, fire protection, service in a civic guard, lighting, and direct political participation—were, over the course of the nineteenth century, transferred to emergent civic and national bureaucracies, and to large-scale political parties. The individual was less and less required to act as a citizen. At the present time only the payment of taxes and occasional jury duty are required of the citizen; voting in elections for candidates in often distant constituencies is usually optional. Service in bureaucratized armed forces is periodically required, but only for short periods of time. The ancient role of citizen has thus become attentuated; the contemporary citizen is likely to be a passive participant, and by virtue of this passivity and the social distances involved, his socialization into citizenship and civic roles is likely to be less binding and less effective. And given the demands for civic socialization, in the fact of the continuous urbanization of the world, the continuous inflow of "peasants" from under-developed rural areas, citizenship in urban areas is weaker today than at any time in the history of cities.

The professionalization of municipal services is based on political and bureaucratic ethics rather than on civic ethics; that is, officials in the modern city restrict their loyalties to that of party or office, rather than serving the city as a whole; and as civic ethics weaken, the professionals seem at times to be less accountable than ever before to any set of public standards. Privacy, in the sense of greed and the rejection of public norms, invades the performance of public roles, whether they be civic, professional, or bureaucratic.[19] The official increasingly tends to serve his own purposes—often illegal—because civic morality and obligation are not pressing role demands.

Where the growth of urbanism was very rapid, civic norms did not develop fast enough or take root deeply enough to serve as the basis of ethical or moral codes that would restrain those whose political and social functions were necessary simply because of the city's size and problems. Thus, professional politicians, bosses, and machines were "necessary" in the nineteenth century; or rather, their services were necessary, despite the fact that neither the public nor its governors had maintained the civic codes that had existed previously when the rate of urban growth was slower. The civic morality of the nineteenth century was weaker than that of earlier centuries. In the twentieth century, civic morality is weak for the opposite reasons. The jurisdictional structures governing conduct are larger than and independent from the constraints of locality.

In the fourteenth century, in resistance to the rise of the bourgeoisie, older feudal classes had begun to celebrate and articulate their ceremonial roles. The Reformation, on theological grounds, fostered the development of privacy by emphasizing either the direct, immediate intercession of God himself or the necessity of the individual to justify himself in his certitude of salvation. The self-probing analysis and concern that had hitherto been reserved for the religious virtuoso under regular monastic Catholicism became incumbent upon masses of the emerging Protestant middle and lower-middle classes. At the same time, the development of capitalism, and later on, of industrialism, and still later on, of bureaucracy, have all resulted in the creation of new formal, public, occupational roles that are impersonal, segmental, and limited in their effects. These roles have been made available and incumbent upon larger and larger segments of the population. But the development of such roles was more rapid among and diffused more pervasively to the middle and upper classes. Therefore these role formations had a differential incidence among the population of the society as a whole. In addition, the growing secularization of society, the destruction of feudal bonds, and the growth of urbanism all have tended to devalue ritual roles for the lower classes. Ritual and ceremonial roles, along with occupational, institutional, technological, and leadership roles, have been appropriated by increasingly large upper and middle classes.

Intimacy in Mass Society

In the decline of traditionalism, intimate roles have become almost a residual category that remains when all other forms of role definition have been removed. But they remain a residual category only because of the biological nature of man—that is, it is necessary for infants to survive a period of intimacy in close proximity to others who are present, continuously and deeply, for long periods of time. And the needs for personal, emotional, undifferentiated gratification, once evoked in early childhood, persist even when the predominance of role behavior governed by these biological needs diminishes in frequency or importance in the total role behavior of the individual. Thus, residual intimate behavior coexists with other types of role behavior among virtually all individuals. But, as we have indicated, it is less important among the middle and upper classes in a society that makes formal objectivity and formal rationality—i.e., the necessity to deal with others on the basis of objective and impersonal standards—a condition for the operation of almost all modern institutions. At the same time, the very classes which benefit materially by their occupancy of roles that require public performance are given the material and some of the intellectual resources to afford privacy. To the extent that the middle and upper classes are given, through the processes of education and socialization, the cultural and intellectual resources to use and enjoy privacy the growth of the size of these classes also emphasizes the importance of private behavior.

Not all privacy, of course, is necessarily used constructively. The ability to fill up the time afforded by privacy has always been a problem in human societies, and as we have indicated, much social ritual is devised to avoid the self-confrontation involved in privacy.

But the development of privacy coincides with the development of public role performance; the two, in modern society at least, are not opposites; rather, they complement each other and in some cases compensate for each other. For one of the major characteristics of public roles is, as we have indicated, that they are segmented; only a limited amount of time is spent in the performance of public roles. The affluence of the official, the segmental nature of public roles, and the various scattered audiences for public roles allow the official actor to withdraw from the public stage and to live, if he is able, in another set of intimate roles, or in privacy, which may be suitable to him if, out of his past, he is able to construct an integrated and unified sense of self.

Economic Individualism

We have argued that the conception of privacy is based on the conception of the person as an individual, perceiving himself psychologically and socially in part separate from social collectivities, though we recognize that no man is an island; one cannot achieve even consciousness of oneself in isolation. Historically, the collectivities which can become so constraining that they deny the possibility of individual consciousness have been the family and the locality. The social pressures which have at times freed the individual from the collectivity have in part been political, in the sense that political segmentation separates both the ruled and the rulers from a common collective consciousness and allows each to see the other as distant and separate from themselves.

Yet the political processes coexist with, and may be less important than, economic processes. In "primitive" societies, economic processes were usually conducted by the family, whether nuclear or extended, within the confines of a restricted territory. The economic actor was an agent of the family and was responsible to and for the family. The family both accepted responsibility for its members and held its members accountable to it. The family was both the political and economic unit, and was held responsible for the action of its members by other families and their agents.

The emergence of the individual, then, took place when individuals were able to separate themselves from the family in economic activities. This must have occurred when technical change, urbanism, and the rise of markets presented new opportunities to which families, primarily oriented to agriculture, were not able to respond. Beyond this, the inevitable dislocations caused by such catastrophes as wars and famine tended to destroy family units as effective economic entities. Individuals, responding to the sense of opportunity produced by social and technical change and by the inability of family units to respond, were able to fill the gaps created by such change. Individual entrepreneurs, artisans, and traders, from the standpoint of traditional and family-based standards, became a disturbing element in history, but more than that, they became individuals. They were eternally outside of traditional structures, often despite their intentions. Younger sons, "upstarts," and the declassed individuals (declassed because they existed outside normal agrarian structures) either attempted to create new family systems, which gave them rights and privileges that older established family systems had already achieved, or attempted to create rights for themselves as individuals. Both processes occurred simultaneously, and both processes overlapped and contradicted each other. In ancient Rome, for example, as has occurred in almost all other societies, new families emerged to challenge the dominance of old families, but having succeeded in

that challenge, attempted to reinstate for their own benefit the traditional rights that older families had enjoyed.

But the opposite strategy—of attempting to achieve rights as individuals, not as family members—became the basis for the emergence of individualism wherever that occurred. Thus, in ancient
Greece the notion of the citizen who had rights as an individual became a reality, even though by the reforms of Cleisthenes the individual received his rights as a member of an arbitrary and fictional
deme, an economic and political jurisdiction.[20] Historically, this
process was not smooth, continuous, or linear; almost every major
era of economic expansion and opportunity works to produce
individualism, and every extended period of economic contraction
tends to produce collectivism. This is merely to say that in periods
of economic contraction families, especially privileged families, have
tended to organize themselves to preserve existing rights and privileges for family members.

In eras of great technical change and economic expansion, the
availability of opportunity limits the desire and ability of families
to maintain their own aggrandizement simply because there seems to
be enough opportunity for everyone, including their scions. Technical change provides opportunity for previously less-favored individuals and families, since the older dominant families tend to define
the prestige of occupations and forms of wealth in terms of the
standards of the past—standards upon which their own prestige was
originally based. Thus, in almost every period of technical change
new opportunities occur in economic areas of low prestige; declassed
individuals and families are allowed to enter these areas, partly because the new activities are not valued socially, and partly because
favored families usually prepare themselves for occupations and
activities that were valued in the past. The individual with nothing
to lose but his past is willing to enter low-prestige occupations if
economic opportunity exists. Yet such individualism does not always
result, as noted, in permanent change, because of the tendency of
successful individuals to institutionalize their success by founding
new families, which in turn become subject to the dynamics of
family aggrandizement.

Only with the rise of the corporation—or more precisely, the
joint stock company—were individuals able to exist "institutionally"
as individuals. With the advent of the corporation, economic rights
and privileges were defined in terms of the rights and privileges of
individual economic actors, not families. Of course, such a develop-

ment rested on the notion that a corporation had a separate existence apart from any one individual, and that within a corporation,
at least in principle, individual accountability could be established.
These innovations developed in the West over a period of more than
half a millennium; they were produced by the rise of accounting,
accountability, and new forms of business law and political and
legal decisions. But while these processes occurred, the businessmen,
the entrepreneurs, fought not only for the legal and political rights
that would make business possible, but also against all forms of legal
and political closure that would restrict their right to act as businessmen and as individuals. One must hasten to add, however, that whenever business dynasties—great fortunes won by powerful individuals—
emerged, the dynasts attempted to institutionalize their achieved
rights by legal and political as well as economic monopolies. The
successful dynast attempted to buy into the older establishments
by acquiring older established rights and duties, by intermarriage,
and by shifting the basis of his wealth to those forms that had
achieved status in the past. Such mobility did not become the basis
for new familistic aristrocacies so long as continuous economic and
technical change prevented the stabilization and enclosure of opportunities at any fixed level. The economic expansion and development
that began slowly in the twelfth and thirteenth centuries in western
Europe, that reached its high point in the nineteenth century, and
that has continued, perhaps unevenly, until the present became the
greatest thrust toward individualism in our society.[21]

But of course the individualism that emerged is not the individualism of laissez-faire capitalism; it is not the individualism of a soli-
tary Robinson Crusoe who makes an economic world out of nothing
on the basis of his own efforts. As units of business activities grew
in size, business became too large to be run by individuals. In the
modern world, large corporations serving mass markets are the dominant unit of organization. As the corporations emerged, the problem became one of fitting individuals into business units that are
supra-individual. What emerged was the bureaucratic role of the
businessman, of the "official," and of the "employee." The business
role—in continuous elaboration, articulation, segmentation, and
specification—was defined by emerging internal "laws" of business,
by personnel codes, by specifications of rights, duties, functions, and
accountability. Such roles were defined by public as well as private
law with reference to fiduciary relationships and criminal offenses,
and in highly specified grounds for firing, hiring, and promotion. The

process is a continuous one. Out of this process came the role of the business official—not one role but thousands of roles.

But collectively these roles became a curious modification of individualism. Business roles have a curious kind of objectivity. They can be treated as a body of law, as a set of requirements, and as codes of conduct. They are separate from the behavior of the individual in the sense that the latter can be judged against the objective standards of a code. But like the demands of citizenship, business roles do not involve the total activity of the individual.* The individual has a private life apart from his business activity. In fact, he is required to have a separate private life. If he mixes his private money with his business money, he is often accused of misappropriation of funds, which constitutes grounds for dismissal, prosecution, or other forms of punishment. If he acts out of personal loyalty or sympathy to the extent that he violates codes of sound business practices, he is subject to perhaps less stringent censure.[22] All such requirements exist in principle; and avoidance of prosecution, as with all crime, is subject to successful evasion of the codes, as well as the willingness and ability of prosecutors to enforce standards that objectively exist. The fact that one can easily recall successful violations of the law does not deny the existence of the law or the fact that violators are frequently prosecuted.

Viewed from the standpoint of the business official, the existence of business roles results in a segmentation of the areas of his life that are bounded by the public and the private. The public role is that of an official; and it is a public role that the official responds to only in some areas of his total life. In dealing with outsiders in his business affairs, he is enjoined to act according to standards that are defined for him by the "company." Moreover, he is often viewed as a representative and as a symbol of the company, especially if he has relatively high office with high public visibility. In dealing with other officials in his company, he is enjoined to act within the framework of his legal rights, duties, and obligations, as defined by the code. In principle he is not supposed to exceed his authority nor to neglect his duty, even when such injunctions can never be clearly or totally specified. He must respond to other officials in his official capacity, though in working with them he may define himself and the others as sharing a common fate and culture that allows him to respond to others as a total human being. He has to judge whether

*Much of this applies not only to business but to all larger bureaucracies.

their common humanity allows him to exceed or minimize the requirements of corporate citizenship and to determine when making allowances for common humanity becomes criminal. Does one protect an incompetent or a criminal violator of public codes who is a corporate friend, out of personal sympathy or friendship; or does one respond to a corporate code in which such protection is a crime?

As an individual outside of the office, in his home, with friends, or in other roles—citizen, lodge member, neighbor—he may be able to project aspects of himself that are not permissible or appropriate in his official role. He may be a drunk, an eccentric or radical, a lecher, or a humanitarian in these personal circumstances.

The individual is always forced in such situations to manage his self-projection so that his behavior in each social position is appropriate to that position. He is constrained not to violate the *situs* of the position he is acting in at the moment. He has to know when the various roles he occupies overlap; that is, if in a nonofficial role he produces behavior that violates the standards of his official roles, he has to judge when the feedback from such behavior will endanger his business role. He thus must know when public drunkenness in his club will be viewed by his bosses as not simply private behavior. He must judge whether employing his incompetent son-in-law in a highly sensitive position is a violation of his public role. He has to reconcile the standards of his multiple roles in such a way as to achieve a balance between these standards. The amount of freedom that is available to him is in part a product of the historic development of his power and the breadth of and overlap between public office and private roles. Given these ambiguities and contradictions in role demands, he must reconcile his willingness to exchange the rewards of role fulfillment with the demands that each set of roles personal and public, places upon him. His willingness to make particular exchanges is in part a function of how he values the rewards of role fulfillment and the alternative rewards that might be available to him if he ignored projected role demands.

In some institutions, historical eras, and social locations the amount of freedom available to an individual in making these choices is relatively great.[23] But under other circumstances the demands of one institution may be so great as to make conformance to a particular set of role demands almost imperative. When they are imperative, one can say that the possibility for privacy is minimal—i.e., the individual's private existence receives no social recognition or opportunity for expression. If the situation is totalitarian, privacy may be banned from consciousness. Individualism and privacy are thus possible only in a pluralistic society where no one set of role demands is overwhelmingly imperative. In the American small town of the nineteenth and early twentieth centuries, the role demands of the business firm tended to be all-embracing, and all other role demands tended to be secondary. Since World War II the demands of the firm have tended to diminish—in part because the firm has become so large that the maintenance of control is more difficult; in part because of an increasing urbanization of life, such that the corporation is partially submerged in the city. Thus, the individual can separate his business life from his private, residential life; he can profit from the anonymity of the city. The corporation can increasingly be less effective in making demands upon the official. As a result, the corporation is forced to be more tolerant. The climate of permissiveness thus has increased not only for the society at large but for the corporate official, though corporate standards remain central to those executives who aspire to the highest levels of leadership. But even here corporate demands are expressed more in terms of fulfilling the corporate role than in taboos governing private behavior. Thus, the demands are for a positive commitment to the corporation rather than a manifest denial of private life. The effects, however, are largely the same.

Notes

1. Bruno Snell, "The Rise of the Individual in the Early Greek Lyric" (chapter 3), in *The Discovery of the Mind—The Greek Origins of European Thought* (Cambridge, Mass.: Harvard University Press, 1953; reprint, New York: Harper Torchbooks, 1960).

The *Oxford English Dictionary* gives the following early meanings of *privacy*: "some time to spare; some privacies and retreats from business; some breathing fits from the affairs of our vocations"; also: "places of retreat (1652)" —*The Compact Edition of the Oxford English Dictionary—Complete Text Reproduced Micrographically* (New York: Oxford University Press, 1971), vol. 2, p. 2306.

2. Jacob Burckhardt, the Individual"—Personality, Glory, Ridicule and Wit" (part 2), in *The Civilization of the Renaissance in Italy*, trans. S. G. C. Middlemore (London: George Allen & Unwin—Phaidon Press, 1945).

3. For the word *private,* the *OED* gives: "withdrawn from public life, deprived of office, peculiar to oneself . . . withdrawn or departed from the public body; by Wyclif applied to the order of the Friars c. 1380."—*OED,* p. 2306.

The declining sense of self characteristic of certain eras is depicted by writers such as José Ortega y Gasset—in his *An Interpretation of Universal History,* trans. Mildred Adams (New York: W. W. Norton, 1973), especially chapters 7 and 8—for ancient Rome. The works of Tolstoy, Dostoevski, and Chekhov describe this decline in the late autumn of tsarist Russia; after the purge of the Russian middle class, individualism went underground as the collective personality affirmed itself.

4. See Alexis de Tocqueville, *Democracy in America,* vol. 1, trans. Reeve-Bowen (New York: Vintage Books, 1945), chapter 17, especially pp. 326 and 328: "No sort of comparison can be drawn between the pioneer and the dwelling that shelters him. Everything about him is primitive and wild, but he is himself the result of the labor and experience of eighteen centuries. . . . It is difficult to imagine the incredible rapidity with which thought circulates in the midst of these deserts. . . . I do not think that so much intellectual activity exists in the most enlightened and populous districts of France."

5. Eleanor Smith Bowen, *Return to Laughter* Garden City: Anchor Books, 1965); Bronislaw Malinowski, *Argonauts of the Western Pacific* (1922; reprint, New York: E. P. Dutton, 1961), chapter 17: "Magic and the Kula," pp. 329 ff., especially p. 401.

For some sociologists, urbanism is a source of the possibility of the cultivation of privacy, in the sense that the density of a vast number of alternatives for varied patterns of social relations allows the individual to abstract himself from any pattern and to select his own combination. This combination may be different for each individual; furthermore, the individual is not subject to the continuous and searching scrutiny of any particular group. If he succeeds in this attempt, to achieve privacy he becomes an individual. Simmel expresses this point of view in his essay on "The Metropolis and Mental Life."

The opposite point of view is that the individual, because of the density of social relations, is separated from all affective (not effective) social relations, is denied the psychological resources to confront the plurality of demands made upon him. He falls apart; his behavior becomes anomic and he is driven in the direction of suicide. Or, in dealing with the absence of social support and social norms, he may submit to the dominance of people and institutions whose strength and authority are so prominent that he surrenders himself to them and denies his individuality. Durkheim expresses the latter view, while a whole literature, perhaps starting with Ortega y Gasset (*The Revolt of the Masses*) reflects the former.

6. Lewis Mumford, *The City in History* (New York: Harcourt, Brace & World, 1961), p. 296: "In the medieval city the spirit had organized shelters and accepted forms of escape from worldly importunity in chapel or convent; one

might withdraw for an hour or . . . a month." See also p. 285: "The first radical change, which was to alter the form of the medieval house, was the development of a sense of privacy." See also pp. 383–84 on privacy as the luxury of the well-to-do.

7. Richard Sennett, *The Fall of Public Man* (1974; reprint, New York: Random House, Vintage Books, 1978), pp. 60–63; 78–80.

8. See Karl Jaspers's trenchant criticism of psychoanalysis in *Man in the Modern Age* (Garden City, N.Y.: Doubleday, Anchor Books, 1957), pp. 166–68. See also Philip Rieff's *The Triumph of the Therapeutic* (1966: reprint, New York: Harper Torchbooks, 1968), pp. 74–76. See especially the writings of Karl Kraus, for example: "There are real psychoanalysts about whom one does not know, for one thing, whether they are doctors or patients; and it is part of the nature of the illness and its therapy that the illness has the therapy and the therapy the illness, that the healthy emerge from the doctor's office as patients and the patients as doctors. Constant confusion prevails there. . . . But it is a sorcery that has no master and must keep engendering only apprentices."—Karl Kraus, "The Sorcerer's Apprentices," in Harry Zohn, ed., *In These Great Times: A Karl Kraus Reader* (Montreal: Engendra Press, 1976), p. 96.

9. See Lionel Trilling, *Sincerity and Authenticity* (Cambridge, Mass.: Harvard University Press, 1971), especially chapters 5 and 6.

10. Paul Radin, *The World of Primitive Man* (New York: H. Schuman, 1953), chapters 1 and 8. B. Malinowski, *Crime and Custom in Savage Society* (New York: Harcourt Brace & World, 1926).

11. Paul Radin, *Primitive Religion: Its Nature and Origin* (1937; reprint, New York: Dover Publications, 1957), chapters 2, 6 and 7.

"True wisdom is only to be found far away from the people, out in the great solitude, and it is not found in play but only through suffering. Solitude and suffering open the human mind, and therefore a shaman must seek his wisdom there."—A Caribou-Eskimo shaman, quoted from K. Rasmussen, *Intellectual Culture of the Caribou Eskimo*. See also Max Weber's *Ancient Judaism* on the prophets, and his essays referred to below.

12. Max Weber, "The Social Psychology of the World Religions" and "Religious Rejections of the World and Their Directions," in Hans Gerth and C. Wright Mills, *From Max Weber* (New York: Oxford University Press, 1946).

13. Max Weber, "Property Systems in Social Groups" (chapter 2), in *General Economic History*, trans. Frank Knight (New York: Collier Books, 1961).

14. See Mumford, *The City in History*.

15. Lawrence Stone, *The Family, Sex, and Marriage in England, 1500–1800* (New York: Harper & Row, 1977), chapter 3.

16. W. G. Forrest, *The Emergence of Greek Democracy 800–400 B.C.* (New York: McGraw-Hill, 1966), chapters 1 and 2, also pp. 191 ff.. See also A. R. Burn, *The Pelican History of Greece* (Baltimore, Penguin Books, 1966), pp. 193 ff.; Morton Smith, *The Ancient Greeks* (Ithaca, N.Y.: Cornell University

Press, 1960), pp. 65 ff.; Max Weber, *The City*, trans. Don Martindale and Gertrude Neuwirth (New York: Free Press, 1958), pp. 169–70.

17. Weber, "Sociological Significance of Civic Unity," in *The City*, pp. 108 ff.

18. Emile Durkheim, *The Division of Labor in Society*, trans. George Simpson (1933; reprint, New York: Free Press, 1964), especially book 1, chapter 7, but also throughout the argument. See also Fustel de Coulanges, *The Ancient City* (translator not indicated) (Garden City, N.Y.: Doubleday, Anchor Books, n. d.), books 2, 3, and 4. Also Henri Pirenne, *Medieval Cities*, trans. Frank D. Halsey (1925; reprint, Princeton University Press, 1969), especially chapter 7: "Municipal Institutions."

19. M. Ostrogorski, *Democracy and the Organization of Political Parties* (New York: Macmillan, 1908); John Thomas Salter, *Boss Rule: Portraits in City Politics* (New York: McGraw-Hill, 1935); Lincoln Steffens, *The Shame of the Cities* (1904; reprint, New York: Farrar, Straus & Giroux, 1957).

20. W. G. Forrest, "The Reforms of Cleisthenes" (chapter 8), in *The Emergence of Greek Democracy* (New York: McGraw-Hill, 1970).

21. Weber, *General Economic History* (chapter 2).

22. Weber, "Bureaucracy," in Gerth and Mills, *From Max Weber.*

23. Marc Bloch, "The Man of Several Masters" (chapter 15), in *Feudal Society*, trans. L. A. Manyon (Chicago: University of Chicago Press, 1961). See also Everett C. Hughes, "Dilemmas and Contradictions of Status," *American Journal of Sociology*, 1 (July 1944–May 1945): 353–59, reprinted in L. Coser and B. Rosenberg, eds., *Sociological Theory, a Book of Readings*, 3rd ed. (New York: Macmillan Co., 1969), pp. 355–65.

Chapter 3

Privacy in Its Social Settings

Physiological privacy and the sense of self are expressed most directly and most crudely in the experience of physical pain and pleasure. Only the individual can directly experience physical pain. By sympathy or empathy he *indirectly* experiences the pain of others. But a far more important kind of privacy is expressed directly through the body. It originates in the sense of self, in the symbolic sphere, but expresses itself in biological terms, in pain or euphoria. The inner workings of the body, one's physiological processes, most often make themselves only dimly present to others, but are almost always present to the self. The individual in control of himself may not convey his sense of pain or well-being to others; as a result, that which is truly private and within his control can come to represent an inner sense of self. It is that part of the sense of self that is truly one's own, truly private, and it is ultimately, as we have noted, incommunicable.

The physical sense of self may be different from self-identity when the latter is the defender of one's self-image or one's total personality—that is, one's tastes, one's internal self-recognition, and one's internalized identification with others—but because of the centrality of the physiological, its closeness to an inner core of mood, sensation and meaning, one can easily equate the total sense of self with those physiological manifestations that are uniquely present to the individual and not necessarily to others. Thus, disturbances in the total psyche of the individual are likely to be transformed into physiological symptoms.

The three major physiological systems that are most available to embody this sense of self are the respiratory, digestive, and cardiovascular systems. A sense of anxiety may alternately present itself as heightened blood pressure, excess perspiration, or gastric disturbances.[1] In extreme cases, such symptoms may take the forms of pseudo heart-attacks, constipation, ulcers, colitis, and flatulence (in the latter case, the symptom is socially projected). They may also be present in shortness of breath, hyperventilation, the gulping of air, or even asthma. All of these symptoms tend to resemble purely physiological disturbances, yet more than a hundred years of psychiatry has allowed us to cconclude that a psychological disturbance often becomes transformed into a physiological one. Among some populations, hysterical anxiety may take the form of blindness and paralysis. Conversion hysteria, the simplest form of anxiety, is the most public.

To reiterate, psychological disorders often take the form of physiological damages that are themselves oppressive. Damages to the ego in social relations, to the superego, to the sense of self-esteem, shame, embarrassment, social isolation, and many other psychological wounds become translated into physical symptoms. The individual concretizes his sense of self in physiological terms. In doing so, he transforms damages to the sense of self that are psychological, vague, and ephemeral into symptoms that are comprehensible as physical pain. Two processes may be possible. The first is the physical; the physiological expression of damage and pain is always more direct and concrete, and does not require an inner, self-conscious recognition of even the fact of psychological damage. Those who by culture or training are not used to abstract conceptualization can experience psychological injury in the most concrete form possible: self-inflicted physical pain or damage. Secondly, the translation of psychological damage, of injury to the sense of self, can be expressed without recourse to the conscious knowledge that the injury is to the sense of self. Thus, one can avoid recognition of one's injury when one does not want to face the fact of that injury. Physiological symptoms may be an attempt to avoid consciously dealing with the fact of psychological injury.

Generalized anxiety, which involves a higher level of consciousness of the sense of psychological injury, is usually experienced
among those who are better educated, or capable of intellectualized
self-awareness; but even among such groups, anxiety is usually
accompanied by physiological symptoms.

But both processes are possible only because at an unconscious
level the individual makes a physiological personification of the core
of a sense of self into the physiologically private.

Social Aspects of Physiological Privacy

But since individuals necessarily live in worlds that inevitably
become social, extremes of private, psychosomatic ailments become
noticeable to, and the object of concern by, others. Moreover, the
transformation of the psychological into the physiological may become the source of psychological warfare against others. For example, if one damages oneself to the extent that he causes others to
worry, to focus their attention on him, to feel guilty, he uses his
private ailment as a social weapon to force others to notice him and
his wounds. But since this process of conversion may not be consciously known to its subject, he does not have to account for his
illnesses; he may simply regard them as given. Since the psychological origins of these illnesses are not known to others, they cannot
blame the ill person for the attention he unknowingly demands or the
pain he causes. Moreover, even if the others know or suspect the
psychological origins of physiological symptoms, they may not want
to risk further damage to the neurotic's sense of self-esteem by
pointing out that at some deeper levels, he is faking it. They may
also know or have learned that the very existence of the physiological symptom is a response to psychological injury, and that the ill
person has a means of resisting self-knowledge. To suggest that the
illness has psychological origins is to run right into this resistance;
in doing so, one may run into a stone wall, incur abuse, or risk
damaging the ill person further. Also, the individual who makes such
a suggestion is placed in the position of being an amateur psychiatrist, a position that many people may not want to accept; at least
they may not want to accept the consequences of such a position.

In these extreme cases of physiological privacy, then, the private
ultimately becomes socialized. In the less extreme cases, both genuine

physical ailments and those that are the result of psychosomatic transformations are endured as part of the cost of maintaining a separate, albeit injured, sense of self. The individual bears his pain internally as part of the uniqueness of his self, as a private world that he experiences directly, although others may be only dimly aware of it. Thus, some neurotics resist therapy because they believe that their neurosis provides their only sense of self. To overcome neurosis is to lose one's identity.

Another physiological system that is the object of psychological transformation is the sexual system. We will deal with this in detail later, and will here confine ourselves to a few general remarks.

The Privacy of the Perverted

Another, and critical, form of privacy surrounds "perverted" behavior. By this we mean that the stigma surrounding certain forms of behavior causes the person to practice that behavior in private, or to avoid expressing his belief in public. To understand the meaning of the privacy of the perverted, one must first state reluctantly some sociological truisms. Every society, whether severe or tolerant in the degree to which it insists upon conformity to its norms, defines some forms of human behavior as intolerable and introduces, at formal or informal levels, taboos and sanctions governing such behavior. The tabooed behavior usually includes some kinds of behavior that are biologically "natural," regardless of social definitions.* Such tabooed behavior may include incest, adultery, voyeurism, exposure, homosexuality, and fetishism. But the taboos need not apply exclusively to sexual deviancy. Excesses of greed, fraud, miserliness, theft, may also be included. Religious deviancy—heresy, schismatic belief, or heterodoxy—can be defined as taboo. In some situations, at some times, or among some people the same behavior or beliefs may be considered permissible or even valued; the fact that they are devalued in particular times, places, or situations makes them socially but not biologically unnatural.

Certain kinds of diseases can be subject to the same kinds of stigmas. Personal uncleanliness and disorder can also be included in our catalogue of bases for stigmatization. Sociologists have reported

---

*By biologically "natural" we mean behavior that in itself is not biologically damaging, and that requires no social definition or label to sustain it.

on the stigma of the cleft palate, on the stigma of blindness and deafness, on the stigma of being a hospital patient in a work-oriented society, on the stigma of senescence, of insanity—all diseases or infirmities that are not contagious. The stigma of contagious disease may of course be related to the desire to avoid contamination, but such stigmatization, if it has a rational basis, should be related to medical knowledge.[2] The stigmatization of noncontagious-disease carriers may be related to ignorance—or more often, to psychic contagion. Psychic contagion may be, in primitive form, contagion by the evil spirit that is believed to produce the disease or infirmity. In more modern form, psychic contagion means the contamination not by disease or infirmity, but by the stigma associated with that disease or infirmity. This can be called *secondary stigma.*[3] One does not want to share, by one's closeness with another, the other's stigma. It is the avoidance of "guilt by association," regardless of the genuineness of the guilt.

Even some forms of neurosis and psychosis can be the object of sanctions and disesteem. In fact, it would be impossible for us to list all the behavior that can become the object of social stigma.

Individuals are reared to avoid beliefs, behavior, and attributes that produce negative evaluations in a given society. To some degree they internalize the norms whose violation produces stigma, and if they practice the behavior in question, acquire a stigmatized belief, or unwillingly acquire a stigmatized personal characteristic they are likely to develop a sense of guilt or shame. A secondary deviance for behavior or characteristics which, despite the sanctions, they exhibit.

Yet no society has ever fully succeeded in stamping out the kinds of behavior, belief, or attributes that it denounces at a public level. Thus, individuals emerge whose personalities are at odds with the public norms of their society. These "deviants," except for psychotics—and even then, not all psychotics—know that the public exhibition of their discretionary behavior will produce sanctions ranging from incarceration or expulsion to the denial of opportunity to achieve the best fruits of social position and esteem within their society. The consciousness of the disesteem attached to deviation from public norms forces them, to the extent that they can control their behavior, either to repress its manifestations or to practice it in secret.

If the repression is carried on at an unconscious level, that repression results in the privacy of neurosis, psychosis, and character disturbances, similar to those which we have already discussed. If the behavior so repressed is done as a result of a conscious attempt to avoid sanctions, it then becomes secret behavior. The individual must consciously cultivate privacy as a concomitant to his practice or belief. A large part of his life must necessarily consist of the avoidance of situations in which he is subject to exposure, and a large part of his behavior must be the projection of appearances and actions that violate his private beliefs or desires.[4] The complexity of his public behavior, as opposed to his private norms, means that a large part of his psychic energy is invested in sidestepping, avoiding, and misleading not only those who are distant from him but those who might otherwise be close to him, but who do not know the form of his perversity. He may be forced to become at some levels of his behavior a social isolate. He must regulate his personality consciously to avoid self-incrimination; he must withhold himself, must lie, deceive, and manipulate others to avoid the disesteem he would receive from open self-expression. And these psychological complexities are doubly and triply complex, because the individual must often pay lip service to some of the public norms he privately rejects, since he usually wants to achieve the benefits that conformity produces.

The burden of privacy in these cases is almost intolerable. The individual is forced to isolate himself from most human contacts, from most of the intimacy that is regarded as normal to the population at large, and to cut himself off from most of the normal pleasures and virtues of sociability. Exceptions will be noted. Even when, at a public level, he practices the public behavior that he in private rejects, he cannot gain the full level of satisfaction that such behavior would produce were he not psychologically so complex. The burden of isolation is so great that from time to time he may be forced to expose himself, to "get caught," to reveal his perversity to friends who do not necessarily share in his behavior. In doing so, he takes the risk of losing those minimal social contacts that may give him the pleasures of "normal" social relationships. Yet the burden of privacy is so great as at times to be unbearable. Perhaps one large reason why the crime rate is so high is that individuals ultimately hope to get caught in order to escape the burden of isolation. Even someone who practices the privacy of repression under the pressure of isolation will "act out" from time to time—the acting out being a release from tension. In doing so, he risks losing not only the social benefits he gains from repression, but the total basis for his self-manipulated personality. To maintain the privacy of perversity, as we have noted, requires the highest levels of self- and personal control, and a spurious rationality that enables the individual to calculate each and every situation in order to estimate the degree to which he can reveal himself. Spontaneity invites sanctions and defeat. Aichhorn, following Freud, claims that a great deal of criminal arrests and incompetence in crime are due to the desire to punish oneself for guilt, due to offenses other than those for which one allows oneself to be caught, to avoid the isolation of deviancy. "Coming out of the closet" may be similarly related to the need to escape the burdens of stigmatic privacy.[5]

In this respect, the person exhibiting the behavior that is socially defined as perverted is no different than the psychopath who makes the self-conscious, pragmatic control of unsublimated impulses the total basis for his existence. The "perverted" individual can find little relief from the burdens of privacy, which become overwhelming. Yet there are many forms of relief potentially available. The person may seek out others who have similar "perversions," and they may form secret societies. Or they may find others who practice different types of perversions and engage in a social exchange: "You tolerate my perversion and I'll tolerate yours." Thus, a netherworld, a "bohemia," may emerge. Such an exchange is fraught with danger, since there are various levels of disesteem in the practice of the various forms of tabooed behavior. Criminals, may be "good Americans" and may taboo communists; and burglars may hate child abusers.

Despite these dangers, secret societies may emerge. These operate at a number of different levels. If they create wholly secret social codes, they may provide a relief from "normalcy," and the participants may console each other to compensate for their collective disesteem. They may develop counterimages, which place positive evaluations on those traits that are publicly disesteemed, and develop some measure of pride to balance their partially internalized self-devaluation. They risk the danger of becoming characterized as a group and thus achieving collective devaluation and stigmatization. In doing so, they may achieve within their own group some of the benefits of intimacy, social exchange, and prestige at the expense of the disesteem in the larger society that the identification with a stigmatized group entails.

When stigmatized groups emerge as recognized social categories, a deviant individual may choose to spend only part of his time with a deviant group and may live his "normal" life in the "square" world.

In the late 1960s such a person was called, by the "true" deviant, a "plastic man." The plastic man who practices normality in his day-to-day affairs, but who lives a secret life, may have a whole secret social world of friendships and intimacies of language, dress, and other cultural patterns that diverge from his "normal" life. He faces the problem of keeping the two worlds separate. He must reject his friends of the deviant world in public, and make it up to them in private. He must apologize for his normal friends to his real friends, and prove that these are just friendships of convenience. But he always risks the dangers of being unable to keep his two worlds apart, and to the extent that he is only partially successful, he causes one or both sets of friends to feel that his behavior is secretive, bizarre, or unfathomable. This, too, may cause pressures to "come out of the closet," though in doing so the deviant risks surrender of whatever gains he believes ensue from "normal" affiliations. The plastic man is disesteemed for his external normality, and for his lack of commitment and loyalty to deviant culture, among those who have deviancy as their norm. Yet among the deviant ingroup, he may also be respected as a virtuoso in "faking it," for his success in "passing" in the square world might balance this lack of total commitment. Whatever the outcome of these dynamics, ambivalence is always a central element.

Such a split—the schizophrenic life among the doubly committed—involves the possibility of becoming caught by one's square friends and losing those values and valued activities which made the split necessary in the first instance. The psychological complexity of deviant behavior is thus socialized.[6] One lives in two or more worlds and must maintain a separation of those worlds.

One of the ways by which some degree of protective coloration for deviant behavior can be achieved is for the totally deviant person to join the temporary permitted deviances of a normal population; the voyeur may have a feast at a wild party, or the alcoholic may be "normal" on New Year's Eve. But such opportunities are rare, and a "closet" deviant may risk revealing that his form of deviancy is "professional" to the "amateurs" who practice their deviancies on the infrequent occasions of socially allowed suspensions of normality. The "normals," after such situations, are likely to recall the professionalism of the deviant, and to redefine their friend, who heretofore had been regarded as one of them. The sophisticated deviant, even in the permitted situation, must thus fake amateurishness. In some circles, an intimacy based on perversity provides for a sense or euphoria, of daring because it is fraught with the danger of being observed by the intruder from the other world. While acting in the square world, the deviant may have, on the other hand, a sense of guilt for enjoying the normal, banal pleasures.

Yet such complexities are far less difficult than those facing the isolated deviant in a totally square world. When deviance is socialized by being centered in a group, deviants may attempt the process of normalization—of propagandizing the square world with the virtues and values of their deviancy, of initially demanding toleration on the basis of their humanity and ultimately demanding the recognition of the virtues and talents associated with their deviance.

If they succeed, the process usually takes generations to achieve. In the meantime, those who undertake this process risk the social stigma, the rebuffs and avoidance, associated with coming out of the closet. Yet such stigma and rebuffs must inevitably be less damaging than the weight of enforced privacy. In the process of transition to the world outside the closet, an exchange is made between present stigma and the promise of legitimate sociability and intimacy.

One of the great accomplishments of psychology—some might argue its greatest—is that the psychotherapeutic interview allows the deviant a permitted area of social release, where the weight of privacy is, for the hour, lifted, perhaps enabling the individual to subsequently practice his tabooed behavior under less pressure than that which he brought to the interview.[7] Whether the release of pressure results in a change of behavior is not so clear; nor is it clear whether the change in behavior that might ensue is positive or negative. Yet what is clear is that therapy can, at least temporarily, result in lifting the burden of value-enforced and socially enforced privacy.

In earlier periods, the confessional and the medical interview may have had some of the same functions, but the priest and the physician rarely had the personal inclination or the doctrinal sanction to provide sufficient toleration or approval to lift the burden beyond minimal levels. Institutionally recognized deviancy, such as transvestism in primitive societies, also helped to relieve the burden of privacy, but it generally removed the practitioner of what otherwise would have been stigmatized behavior from the possibility of living a normal life and enjoying its pleasures. In a similar way, the toleration of the deviant by groups whose organizing principle is something other than deviance is tinged with condescension. Thus, an established upper class will permit some of its members to practice forms of deviancy that it does not in principle approve because they are members of the class: "He may be a homosexual, an alcoholic, or a radical, but he is one of our own." An officer corps, or the elite in any institution, may be tolerant in similar ways, but always the deviant is well aware that he is trading on the power, the prestige, and the bounty of that elite, and always, he "owes" his knowing peers. This may provide him with a minimal cover for his deviancy but not the esteem of his peers.

Normal Deviancy

Our excursion into the world of the deviant and the perverted has been made merely to describe one kind of privacy, a privacy that protects the individual from the prying eyes of others who would devalue him if they really knew him. In such extreme cases, privacy is designed to protect the self, even if that self is fragmented, wounded, or at war with itself. Yet the burdens of this privacy are great. In many cases, they are so great that the individual may risk, wittingly or unwittingly, the danger of stigma, incarceration, degradation, to overcome his overwhelming sense of isolation.

Our excursion has not been another attempt to enjoy the voyeurism of the normal in spying upon the antics of the deviant—by now a nationwide game—but rather has pointed out aspects of privacy that are also present in all normal situations.

Freud's perhaps most famous prudish statement (echoing St. Augustine)—that between feces and urine we are born—meant that biologically we all exhibit behavior that subsequently becomes subject to social disapproval. The human being at birth is subject to appetites that are uncontrolled, amoral, and immoral. He starts with, develops, and channelizes forms of greed, lust, and other biological drives that society disapproves of and frequently bans.[8] He develops patterns of reaction-formation that in themselves are often as much disapproved of as the behavior originally suppressed or repressed. But always the individual must live with his biological inheritance. He develops unattractive illnesses; he needs to eliminate, he passes gas, he sweats and stinks; in addition, he may develop compulsions to be sloppy or filthy, he may eat wolfishly; he loses his temper, he may rant and rave; he develops qualities of either miserliness or profligacy; he may be subject to promiscuity or to irrepressible sexual urges. The catalogue of sexual disorders alone is large enough to fill multivolume encyclopedias. And more generally, the list of socially disapproved behavior is simply inexhaustible.

To repeat, we who are "normal"—like the "pervert"—encounter resistances to our socially disapproved appetites, and produce the same types of reaction-formations: the products of primary disapproval, which become secondary normality. The development of the self forces us to create areas of privacy that are not subject to invasion. Such areas of privacy allow us to free ourselves from overwhelming social constraints on the drives and tendencies that are part of our biological make-up and the process of growth.

Given the process of reaction-formation; most of us never achieve full, ideal maturity. At any rate, we cannot altogether escape our biological origins. The development of a fully articulated social code places demands upon us that would imply complete socialization, but it is rarely achieved. As opposed to sanctions on extreme deviancy or perversion, those on most normal behavior are not as extreme. Yet slights and cuts, disesteem, denial of otherwise available opportunities—in short, the denial of full acceptance—are normal parts of the social process. Most social sanctions occur at the entry points to favored circles; toleration of disesteemed characteristics is usually achieved only after full entry into the circle. Yet in most of our activities it is incumbent upon us to observe the existing etiquette of social relations regardless of how formalized and distant from the inner self such etiquette may be. All of this means that it is necessary for us to manipulate our behavior in order to present ourselves in ways that are consistent with the eitquette and tolerance of relevant social groups. Thus, some degree of deception is necessary, whether that deception is defined as good taste, as manners, as proper behavior, or as an ethical imperative. Manners and other forms of conventional behavior are not only a means of "getting along," of gaining prestige or social acceptance, but are also a means of preserving our sense of privacy. The transformation of socially disapproved thoughts and ideas into socially accepted styles of expression helps us maintain distance from those others whose surveillance would allow us to be seen as we really are. Only when we get to know another person closely do we relax our manners, and show the other what we are in private, as intimates. Thus the suspension of formality, of good manners, of niceness and sweetness, is more often a sign of love, friendship, and closeness than is the presence of "civilized" traits.

Privacy is a necessary attribute for the emergence of a self, for resistance to the total demands made upon the self by others—especially when there is a plurality of others making conflicting demands—and for the necessary adjustment of those aspects of the self that do not find immediate social approval. At the same time, the individual with a strong sense of self always risks estrangement from others, if and when he reveals aspects of himself that violate the norms and expectations of others, either as individuals or as members of groups. It does not matter that the others are subject to similar biological pressures and have their own patterns of reaction-formation that also make them "all too human." The biological expressions of self may be different for particular individuals, and the patterns of reaction-formation may also be different and conflicting. Moreover, in most social situations, we lack the knowledge of others that would enable us to project appropriate behavior to those aspects of their selves that are not immediately revealed. We may lack the time to know one another; or we may sense that greater knowledge might not produce—at least initially—either approval or confirmation of our own sense of self as it exists at a given moment. The social, in any given situation, always expresses less than the self; and since we know this, either consciously or intuitively, we tend to express less than our total selves in any given situation. As a result, the unresolved or unexpressed segments of the self may force us into forms of secrecy that produce a sense of social isolation, of estrangement, of inability to express ourselves as we feel ourselves genuinely to be. And this is likely to be extreme when we are newcomers to those segments of society whose social expectations are highly standardized.

Thus, privacy can always be felt as a burden, even though some forms of privacy are necessary to rescue the self from oversocialization that would deny prior selves, biological heritage, and special patterns of reaction-formation. And this ambiguity, this contradiction in the meaning of privacy and its relationship to the self, is an essential aspect of the human condition. Extreme privacy may result in or be psychosis, and somewhat less extreme privacy may result in overwhelming burdens and internal pressure. But extreme socialization may result in the denial of the self, of the biological and the psychological make-up of ourselves as historical individuals living through time, and not in isolated moments in time. The immanence and power of "the social" may lead us to deny deeply internalized tastes, preferences, values, and standards, which themselves are the product of prior socialization but which have been internalized to

the point where they have become the basis of the self. The surrender of one's sense of self to the social by an individual who has
a previously developed sense of self is a form of psychic suicide.
But to live as a social isolate may become an awesome burden. Between this Scylla and Charybdis, individuals who have developed a
strong sense of self are forced to live.

Sexuality as Privacy

The expression of sexuality, at least in fulfillment, is conventionally far more social than is the operation of the other physiological
systems. Yet in most eras, because of taboos on public expression
of manifest sexuality, sex has been regarded as far more private or
intimate than are most other physiological systems. In any case, the
sense of a sexual self (not sexual identity—the latter refers to identification with a sex, not a self) is subject to the same kinds of transformation as are the other systems. That is to say, damage to the
ego, to the sense of self, can easily translate itself into impaired functioning of one's sexual system. Priapism, premature ejaculation,
impotence, promiscuity, nymphomania, frigidity, and other problems may all be sexual equivalents of other disorders. Damage may
occur to the physiological functioning of the sexual system itself,
or such damage may become socialized; that is, the system may
fail to function properly even though there is nothing organically
wrong with it. The centrality of sex as a source of pleasure and as a
source of the sense of self has undoubtedly led us to believe that
sex is a primary source of the self, as in Freudian theory. Yet once
we recognize the symbolic importance of the transformation of the
sense of self into cardiovascular, gastric, and respiratory systems, as
well as sexual functioning, there is no reason to regard sex as more
"primary" than the other physiological systems, or even more
primary than the sense of self. Certainly extreme disturbances in the
cardiovascular system and the respiratory system (in the case of
asthma) can be more damaging, and disturbances in the gastrointesti-
nal system can produce more obvious physiological symptoms,
though probably less obvious than those produced in conversion
hysteria. But the focus in Judeo-Christian religions on both the
pleasure-producing aspects of sex and their denial has led Western
psychiatrists to make sex and sexual functioning the primary source

of the self, and to make all other psychosomatic (and psychological) symptoms derivative of this major, single cause.

If it is true that impairments in the major physiological systems are the products of a damaged ego, of a damaged sense of the self, then the causes of impaired sexual functioning are of no greater psychological importance than the causes of damage to the other physiological systems. In all of these systems, the central processes appear to be the tendencies of individuals to introject into them their sense of self. Damage, is experienced privately in physiological form. Of course, this is not always the case. Although pure anxiety is likely to have some physiological components, usually in the form of increased respiratory or cardiovascular action, the dominant form of pain may occur at more intellectualized levels, including indecision, rumination, the loss of concentration, and a pure sense of intellectualized frustration. At other extremes, the sense of anxiety may present itself only in the loss of affect, the loss of sleep, and a generalized feeling of estrangement from others. In these cases, when the physiological symptoms are not the dominant ones, the sense of privatization of the pain and the damage to the sense of self are paramount. All of these can be summarized by the term *alienation*— alienation from self and from others. Such alienation results in the sense of self as a void.

Psychosis as Privatization

In the above cases, we have been dealing with some forms of neurosis, as related to the physiological privatization of damages to the sense of self. The process is far more easily understood with psychosis. Some types of psychosis, particularly catatonia, consist of the total internalization of deep disorder such that virtually no communication with others is possible; and, one might add, at times it appears that the individual is unable to communicate with himself. Whatever virtues there are in the sense of privacy, total privatization in the psychological sphere may be deemed insanity. Total privatization in the social sphere would almost inevitably lead to death; if one were to cut oneself off from the social and physical services that sustain life, one would be committing suicide. While this may seem to be extreme, there are hundreds of ways in which self-damaging forms of privatization in the social sphere lead to private impairment.

Whereas catatonia is perhaps the extreme case, hebephrenia retains elements of sociability, but in forms that are so deranged that they may be viewed as simple, uncontrolled emanations of the private, not really social at all. Other forms of insanity result from the privatization of social stimuli so that the meanings are either understood only by their holder or so deranged that they are not accessible to any available system of socially understood meanings that exist in a social cultural environment. Thus, paranoia may be social in its expression ("the man with the Black Box is trying to control my mind") and social in its consequences ("I will kill him first"). But this system of ideational transformations renders the meanings expressed as totally private phenomena, so private that in fact the individual to be "cured" must first become aware of the conventional meanings that surround the origins of his disorder. When he does, he will have little recourse to such privatized systems. Thus the process of therapy, if it works at all, must be such as to destroy the purely private system of thought and to introduce, at a meaningful level, the prevailing conventional systems of thought into the consciousness of the patient to the extent that the patient can deal with others in terms of their systems of thought. "Sanity," of course, does not mean, as we have previously indicated, that the intellectual and cognitive processes of the individual have to be so socialized that the purely private ceases to exist; rather, it means that the individual can translate the noncommunicable feelings of his deep inner self into social terms, which are made available to others and to himself in socially objective forms of language and into action even when he does not (or cannot) understand the deep inner core of his own unconscious.[9]

The extreme cases reveal far more pervasive systems of extreme privatization, which impair the normally "genuinely private" as well as the social. In less extreme cases, various forms of schizophrenia and schizoid behavior result in cryptic clues to such thought systems, which are rarely communicated to others. The cryptic language and clues may be received as eccentricities, or may be accepted without inquiry by others, since further inquiry may open up dangerous "cans of worms" or complexities in social relationships that may be more time-consuming or require more effort than the value of the social relationship is worth. We therefore tolerate each other's schizophrenia as long as the proportion of schizophrenic system to conventional communication is low enough not to damage a social relationship. Moreover, if we are able to share in another's delusional system, we may not feel that the delusional system is damaging to a social relation. This is also true if we can decipher the delusional system. One of the talents necessary for psychiatry is the ability to enter the patient's delusional system without becoming a victim of it and to teach the patient first to translate it into conventional terms. To some degree, we all do this in our normal social relations, though in normal relations with others who are important to us we all risk being entrapped in the delusional system.[10]

Privacy in the Family

The development of private delusional worlds occupies an increasing proportion of the total intellectual life of the schizophrenic or schizoid individual. When it does, he may not be able to discern those systems of meanings, whether conventional or private, communicated to him by others. In extreme cases, each member of a family will be the bearer of a particular private system, and none will be able to communicate with another, except through minimal clues. At some levels, their respective private systems of delusion do not impinge upon each other, and therefore do not disturb one another. At the same time, the level of support that one family member can get from another is necessarily limited. Each member is too involved in his own private system to be able to support the other. Within a family, two or more persons may often share a common private system or systems of delusions, excluding the others. Such shared systems of delusional intimacy depend on the amount of psychic estrangement and guerrilla warfare within the family.

But the same dynamics of privacy may occur at less pathological levels—less pathological in the sense that the members involved in the behavior may be conscious of their withholding themselves from one another. Estranged family members, a married couple, or children and parents may consciously withhold themselves from communication with others or may refuse to project parts of themselves to others in order not to face the confrontation that they know would ensue if they presented themselves fully and openly to the other. This withholding of the self is different from the normal process of social exchange, where one does not reveal all of oneself to others, in that the withholding occurs in situations where previously a fuller disclosure of the self was the norm. Thus, the avoidance of self-projection is a device to preserve a social relationship that has become partially damaged in the hope of avoiding further damage. The partner of the person withholding himself from previously achieved levels of intimacy may be unable to understand the new forms of privacy. He may feel that this withholding of the self is an act of hostility or a product of other substitute relationships of intimacy that exclude himself or herself, or he may feel that his dyadic partner is becoming sick. This is especially true when the new privatization occurs suddenly. If it occurs over long periods of time, the individual may habituate himself to an altered form of a social relationship with an intimate other without ever being aware of the change. Of course, when a drastic act like desertion, an act of violence, or a traumatic outburst occurs, only then is the individual likely, in such altered social relations, to inquire into the origins of the gradual changes leading up to the drastic act. Such "normal" techniques of avoidance may be mutual and subliminally understood, so that a whole etiquette of avoidance is erected on the basis of unstated rules.

For example, a wife may never inquire about the philandering behavior of her husband; the puritanical parent may never inquire into the sexual escapades of his daughter; or a married couple may not want to face the fact of open estrangement or the possibility of divorce and all its problems. They may by slow degrees, even after a traumatic episode, alter their relationship to each other without discussion and perhaps even without an awareness of the change in their behavior. If they do so at a subliminal level, they may reconstitute the very basis of their relationship. But it is possible to do so only because each partner respects the new lines, the new privacy, the new avoidances of each other. The subliminal agreement to respect the privacy of the other can be based on elaborate but unstated rules, which constitute an intricate social relationship. But the very complexity of such a system maximizes the amount of privacy each participant allows the other, no matter how satisfactory the social relationship or the privacy is to the parties involved.

Shared Privacy

In not inquiring into the withdrawal behavior of the other, each participant in these rituals of privacy is clearly aware of what aspects of his behavior or communication could offend the other, and each may be aware that the other is aware, so that the practice of restriction of communication requires high levels of cooperation. But such cooperation must be achieved without an explicitly conscious working out of the rules under which the parties cooperate. Each party must be able to have noted, in previous situations, the taboos, avoidances, values, and sources of trauma and outrage in the other, and, having internalized such images of the other, cuts for himself what emerges as a clear but dangerous path. This is because the patterns of avoidance coexist with intense social communication, often intimacy, on other topics. In addition, both parties become adept at noting the subliminal clues of self-presentation in the other; the distant approach of anger, of distress, of desire for avoidance is communicated far in advance of the presentation of the manifest topics subject to the rules of avoidance. A slight pursing of the lips, a narrowing of the eyes, a frown, perhaps undetectable to outsiders, defines the limits of the area of safety in conversation and social interchange. In these normal cases the avoidance of communication is subject to high degrees of sensitivity to the other, the ability to anticipate the response to one's probable communications and to communicate precisely and in advance one's probable response to unwanted communication. The avoidance of communication in such situations may be one of the highest forms of communication behavior; by it, each party enters a silent contract to preserve the privacy of the other. More direct communication could result in needless confrontation, agony, and the necessity to suspend, as the result of the conflict, all communication.

These processes of rational avoidance are qualitatively quite different from the processes that occur in "schizophrenic" families. In the former, not only is the ability to project communication not impaired by the overwhelming predominance of the private, but the ability to receive communication is equally unimpaired. In the schizophrenic family, the process of correcting the pathology may well be one of "teaching" the members to talk to each other, to develop objective frameworks that overcome the cryptic relationship of their communication. But it also involves the possibility and the necessity of confrontation. The ability to face one another may produce anger based upon the revelation of past injuries, hostility, and the sense of victimization. Perhaps only by going through the trauma of confrontation can the existence of a social objectivity be attained, but the risks of uncontrolled anger and hostility are necessary costs of such a process. In normal social relations where sensitivity-restricted communications are the norm, the social relationship may continue at reasonably satisfactory levels indefinitely, or until perhaps out of a desire to avoid the psychic costs of maintaining high levels of self-control and tactfulness a party may reveal or blurt out the tabooed topic and end the relationship. In fact, in such situations "honesty" may be the means by which one reintroduces a manifest desire to terminate the relationship. Reopening the tabooed topic, the source of basic disagreement, is an implied request for confrontation, the maximization of differences, and the invocation of all the disagreements that had had to be repressed in order to perserve the relationship in the past. The results of such reinvocations may be either to alter the rules of the game or to restructure the area of tabooed and permitted topics, and, at least on a temporary basis, substitute the intimacy of conflict for the isolated privacy that often occurs even within an intimate relationship.

Privacy as Avoidance Patterns

Again, it must be stressed that maintenance of such social relations is possible only when sensitivity, tact, and self-control are present, and all of these place a strain on the individual who must hold back the full flow of his thought or preoccupation. An additional cost may be the sense of isolation that such tact entails, for it is precisely the most important topics governing the relationship between the parties that must be avoided.* The very exercise of such ceremonial avoidance entails a sense of isolation from precisely those from whom one in the past did want to be isolated, but the consequences of rejecting the avoidance may cause an even greater social estrangement. When the burden of avoidances becomes too great, one may blurt out the "truth," but in such cases the blurting out is, at least unconsciously, the result of a desire to end the social relationship.[11]

*Where the necessity of avoidance of tabooed topics places a great strain on the individual and produces a further sense of estrangement from those who are particularly important to one, then the necessity of developing an alternative peer group or friend to whom one can express otherwise suppressed material becomes all-important. Thus, the development of intimacy is a consequence of excessive privacy in another sphere of one's social relations. This is part of the dynamics which result in the creation of peer groups and is certainly a constituent of deep personal friendship. Intimacy is thus a psychological complement to internally forced privacy.

In all of this, it may be noted that the truth so blurted out may not demolish the other, nor may it necessarily produce hostility, confrontation, and social estrangement. Both parties to the ceremonies of avoidance may operate on the assumption that the taboos will produce such dire consequences that they must be avoided at all costs. The final revelation may, however, produce anger, recrimination, mutual recriminations, self-pity, and ultimately a sympathetic understanding of the weaknesses in each other by both parties. The result may be a reconciliation, which usually will be followed by new patterns of avoidance, including the avoidance of the charges and countercharges that have come out in the confrontations. But the basic problem remains that in advance of revealing the "hidden" to the other one does not know the consequences of blurting out the "truth," and if the ceremonies of avoidance have been followed for any length of time they have been followed because of fears that may ultimately prove to be unfounded. In the absence of such foreknowledge, the ceremonies of avoidance produce their own rich subculture.

Privacy Within Organized Social Groups

We argued in Chapter 1 that every social group creates and stresses standards for public and social behavior, and attempts to impress these standards upon its members or the population subject to its social jurisdiction and sanctions. The nature of the public norms, the extent to which they cover the total range of behavior of the populace subject to them, and the extent to which an individual can escape from their immediacy are functions of both the power and the organization of the group. A local community or a peer group may be "totalitarian" in power but relatively narrow in the numbers of people it attempts to influence. In addition, such collectivities as the peer group and community tend to be informal in their organization, resting on their membership to project and enforce their standards on one an another.

Large-scale organizations, on the other hand, by virtue of their size, rest on professional staffs—personnel relations or morale offices —on generalized leadership, or on diffused house intellectuals to create and enforce standards, that is, to define roles and enforce role performance. Beyond this, enforcement of appropriate behavior is sanctioned through internal codes, through private law, and through judicial and bureaucratic courts and procedures attached to the organization.[12] In large-scale organizations the official morality is explicit and codified. In addition, adherence to public morality is a condition for promotion, advancement, and attainment and retention of whatever privileges the organization offers, including, in religious organizations, the possibility of salvation.

All of this means that the private individual, confronting the total organization, encounters officially enforced standards of behavior, morality, and loyalties, which are external to him—compulsory in the sense that it is sanctioned—and which are a medium for either his advancement or the maintenance of his organizational and social positions. If the individual is totally socialized to the goals and values of the organizations to which he belongs or aspires to belong, the goals and values will not appear to be external to him, since the very process of socialization has made these goals and values his internalized perceptual framework. The internalized organization is in fact the self through which he views himself and others. Such an individual is not alienated, though it may be difficult to describe him as an individual. If one disagrees with the values of the organization, one calls the process of deep socialization "brainwashing." If one shares those values, then one sees in the process "the reconstruction of divided selves," which is the goal of all romantic totalitarianisms. Yet successful total socialization is not the problem of modern societies, except, as noted, when we imagine its being done by our enemies, the totalitarians. In most cases, socialization of such depth is not achieved, and the failure of such achievement is regarded as a source of alienation, estrangement, identity problems, and multiple consciousnesses. To be sure, these "modern" problems are the result not only of failures in deep socialization but also of the plurality of agencies that operate upon an individual. Each agency attempts to socialize its members to its behavior codes and values, with no one organization having the jurisdiction and sanctions, along with the means, to monopolize the exclusive socialization of would-be members or subjects to its behavior and value codes.

When an organization is only partly successful in its attempts at socialization, the organization and its values are seen as external to the individual, in opposition to one's sense of one's self as an individual. The organization denies one his own sense of individuality and is inimical to one's privacy.

Of course, in any large-scale organization the distribution of individuals and levels of staff varies with respect both to the organization as a whole and to the place of the individual in it. In some segments or levels of the organization, the emphasis on corporate codes of behavior, on its rhetoric and values, is highly concentrated and dense. The public culture, at these levels, reflects organizational goals, purposes, media, and language, technologies, and symbols of the organization. The private individual in such a situation is likely to see this culture as an oppressive weight bearing down upon him if he is unwilling to accept total commitment and socialization to the organization. In such situations, moreover, the sanctions for resisting total incorporation will be heavy. To be sure, a cynical operator may master all these symbolic and technical systems and may be able to express himself in terms of the culture, even while resisting it, either to save his "self" or to be more effective in advancing himself through the organization. In the latter case, the individual must develop a divided self, a sense of total privacy, which does not allow for public expression of the other self or selves which control either his cynical self or that self which resists the public climate and standards of the organization.

The areas where the public culture is most intense and most likely to be a social imperative are usually in the middle and upper-middle levels of any organization. It is in these areas where the struggle to "make it" to the top is most intense, and the penalties for nonconformity are felt to be the strongest. At the very top, individuals who have "made it" can feel free to express, even in jocular terms, their freedom from the constraints of organization, but such expressions of freedom rest upon the fact that the individual so expressing himself has gone through the rigors and discipline of conformity and has demonstrated in the past his loyalty, commitment, and subservience. By misreading his "nonconformity" as a serious expression of the self rather than as humor, an aspirant to the heights that the "nonconformist" has achieved would endanger his own career.[13]

At every level, those who aspire to mobility must develop a sensitivity to the special culture of an organization and must display their adherence by projecting, through their words and behavior, that culture. This means that the official culture, while concentrated in density in some social locations in the organization, reverberates at less density throughout the organization.

But there are areas where the official culture and morality are despised and rejected. Such hostility is most concentrated in the lower levels of any organization, especially among those groups and classes which, by virtue of age, lack of qualification, or prior commitment, have no hope of reaching the positions whose achievement is secured by, among other things, the expression of public culture. At these levels, another culture invariably evolves. The dominant public culture here is a counter-culture. It takes the "official" culture and transvalues it, making its symbols a source for parody, satire, mockery, and scorn. In these areas adherence to the public organizational culture may be experienced by others as dissent from what emerges as a public counter-culture. Thus individuals at the lower levels of an organization who wish to rise risk alienating their peers, who, having rejected the public culture, see adherence to it as a betrayal. To the aspiring individual, the immediately prevailing counter-culture is an alien, external entity which must be resisted; yet if he wishes to live with a minimum of comfort in his immediate environment, he must find some means of neutralizing the counter-culture while expressing commitment to the culture characteristic of the personnel and staff levels which he has not yet achieved. This has been called "anticipatory socialization." This too is fraught with dangers, the same kinds of dangers that are experienced by those whose major work life is experienced at the levels where official culture is stressed and celebrated.

Privacy and Public Culture

In both areas, a deep tension exists between the public values and the sense of self. Privacy is required simply because the expression of an inner self would place one at odds with one's cultural environment. The extent to which privacy is required, however, is a function of either the weight and force of the sanctions that enforce conformity or the desire of the individual to achieve the values offered by the agents of the dominant culture, whether it be the official culture or the counter-culture. If the individual strongly embraces the sanctioned public values, then he must repress all signs of deviancy. His sense of isolation, his compulsory privacy, is then maximized. These requirements may go even beyond the requirements of public performance, if and when the individual feels that any expression of his sense of self may destroy his public position. Thus, anxiety may intensify conformity rather than rebellion, and such anxiety increases the sense of isolation, the need for privacy.

When the weight of enforced privacy is too great, the individual may seek out others who, through their mask of conformity, seem to reveal another sense of self that allows for the release of un-stylized self-expressions that violate the public norms and public morality, whether official or counter-cultural. Thus, at both levels intimate groups will tend to emerge which allow the expression of selves and values that are denied by the prevailing dominant cultural groups at their level or segment of an organization.

These groups may constitute themselves as cliques, gangs, social circles, social networks, or friendship groups. Some may be so organized as to resist or attack the dominant culture and groups at their organizational level. Their ability to do so depends in part on the power of the dominant group to repress deviant social and cultural systems. In the absence of complete power, such cliques, gangs, and friendship groups may exist at recognized, semiofficial levels, as quasi-organizations or near-groups within organizations that espouse opposing values. They are tolerated because the dominant groups* may not have the power to squelch all opposition or because the cost of repression may deflect the organization from its principal manifest tasks. Beyond this, the toleration of some deviancy may be viewed as permissible since it allows dissidents to perform their manifest task while threatening the system in only minor ways. Deviancy thus reconciles the deviant to the organization and culture which, in principle, he rejects.

The deviant within the organization may also provide the organization with access to and understanding of opposition to the organization, the deviancy "from without." The deviant in this way becomes a resource for social intelligence. Moreover, the employment of a conspicuous deviant may provide the organization with the ability to present a symbolic confirmation of respect for the values of deviants without having to embrace the deviancy itself. This is often called "tokenism," possibly one of the most popular parlor games of American society since the 1960s. Finally, the existence of "staff deviants" provides a potential resource for new leaders and staff if and when the deviant values and culture become so important that the organization must express its recognition of or adherence

---

*Of course, members of the dominant groups may have their own sense of privacy, their own deviancies, and may belong to cliques, gangs, and deviant groups even when "repressing" others under the banner of public morality.

to newly emerging or dominant values. It may do so by promoting and upgrading its own internal reserve or staff of deviants.

But deviancy within "the system" by the self-regarding individual as the achievement of the expression of a private self, in opposition to the public values of the organization, is only one method among many of retaining a sense of self. By far the most frequent form of private opposition is accomplished by psychological withdrawal from the cultural demands of the organization. This involves acceptance of the culture at minimal, formal levels; it means more the compliance with than the acceptance of the public norms. But in the act of compliance the individual makes or attempts to make his nonwork life the locus of his "real" self. He can do so by cultivating a private life outside of work, a sense of another self, of other interests, avocations, and pursuits that give him personal gratifications not expressed in the public life of an organization. In this respect, the family, personal friendships, and peer groups may be of prime importance. If the individual attempts to enlarge the area of a personal privacy without access to the social support provided by others, he may increase his sense of isolation and estrangement by bearing its total weight himself. For all but a few, this is an extremely difficult task. He is more likely to seek—in his nonwork or nonorganizational life—a group of peers, organized on a group or social basis, which not only provides group support to his personal and private values but provides social and cultural density for those values. If he succeeds, the individual may create a bifurcated social life. In one area he offers minimal compliance to externally imposed codes and values, and in another area he may voluntarily embrace others and a culture that he feels expresses a truer self. In the latter case, the individual exposes himself to a new set of external codes, norms, values, and constraints, which may be acceptable because they agree more with his inner interests and values. If, however, he discovers that these other external constraints are inhibiting, he may find only partial freedom from the sense of estrangement that he experiences in his dominant work organization. It is not at all surprising that individuals solve this higher-order problem by adhering to a multiplicity of organized and informal groups, organizations, cliques, friendship groups, and social networks, each of which may provide gratification for some values, some interests, and some opportunities for commitment.

Each set of commitments may be a device that limits the commitment to any one other group, but the total of such commitments may not provide the individual with a sense of the unified self, a unified commitment which expresses his private self and allows him to escape the total sense of estrangement, an estrangement not only fron one dominant group but from all dominant groups. Such an individual may feel that he has parceled out his soul to many others but has passed over himself.

In such cases the individual may feel he has succeeded in freeing himself from the dominant demands of any particular other or group, but the freedom he achieves is the freedom to maintain his distance, not a freedom to realize himself as a unified, integrated personality. Whether such a solution is a solution at all is problematic. The alternatives, of course, may be either the acceptance of and submission to one dominant environment, that is, becoming a "one-dimensional man," or becoming a Nietzschean superman, a romantic hero above and beyond all social claims, who creates and maintains his own value-commitments against the entire world.

Privacy and Total Institutions

Whether in fact the solution of creating alternative social worlds within which a private self can dwell is available is, of course, a function of the dominance of social institutions. One social institution may be so dominant that its reach extends beyond the work or organizational life of the individual, penetrating into all potential alternative milieux that might be available for the construction of alternative selves. Such an organization, whose dominance extends over all facets of the life of an individual, has been called a "total institution." A prison is so pervasive in surrounding the life of an inmate that the individual can only reconstruct his life within its walls. Organizational density in a total institution coexists with cultural density. But let us not rely on such extreme cases as prisons or mental institutions.[14]

A military base that is distant from an urban center, a university town, and a hospital complex all can be so embracing, both within and without the framework of their organizational, social, and cultural reach, that they can surround the total life of an individual. A small town may have the same effect as a company town, a city dominated by one firm; special-purpose cities dominated by single governmental or industrial institution's may be the centers of a dominant cultural and a dominant organization. The network of gossip and familiarity, and the presence of organization personnel all geared to the same value and behavioral standards, constitute a framework and a culture that make the central norms and standards apparently inescapable. In these situations the external cliques and friendship groups all have the same characteristics as the internal cliques within a dominant organization.

But beyond this, certain networks of social institutions may be extremely intense, even though the members of those networks may be widely dispersed throughout a nation. The graduates of West Point are never in one place at the same time, even at the Army–Navy game; but the network of gossip, of mutual and third-party reporting of behavior, serves to provide the total network with some of the same kinds of controls that a small town or an executive suite might provide.

Finally, adherence to a total institution may be voluntary. Its members and alumni may choose to orient their behavior to one another so that they accept the values, the codes, the rhetoric, the symbols of adherence, even though they are widely dispersed, to the extent that this acceptance is based on prior socialization at a deep level, and the concentrated existence of a supporting group to confirm and enforce the values of that group may not be necessary. In such situations the opportunity for privacy, deviancy, and nonapproved intimacy may however be greater than in bounded total institutions.

Privacy in Totalitarian Societies

The "objectivity" of the public world and the denial of privacy and of private worlds is almost by definition assumed in the word "totalitarian." In the societies we conventionally refer to as totalitarian, there is—at any moment—a dominant public ideology, which is usually rigidly codified and subdivided, its elements minutely categorized and explicated. There are formal and informal agencies of control, which, so far as their efficiency permits, scrutinize the actions and lives of individuals. There is also a system of sanctions, which stresses, by the stringency of its sanctions, extreme demands for conformity. Whether the ideology is equally operative on all segments of the society, whether the sanctions are equally applied and the punishments equally administered—these are empirical questions which have to be resolved in each particular case. But the term "totalitarian" in comparison to nontotalitarian societies implies a relatively high probability that extremes in demands on performance and extreme sanctions are stressed.

Viewed from the standpoint of the individual in such situations, every public action or utterance and every inference that others can make from his words or actions makes him subject to the ideological code and the sanctions deriving from it. There is the likelihood that no area of one's personal and private life is exempt from these standards.

Again, there is the possibility that the level of prior indoctrination, brainwashing, or socialization may appear to make every possible thought and action so deeply implanted that the individual remains unaware of the fact that he conforms to repressive standards. Yet such deep socialization seems hardly possible; in the course of a lifetime, the individual will see that the actions or symbols that are indicators of conformity to standards are reversed, quite often dramatically or drastically, either because of changes in the party "line" or because of changes in personnel, usually because of both. The changes require him to alter his behavior, speech patterns, patterns of loyalty, and patterns of commitment to others.[15] In order to make such changes, the individuals, at some psychological level, has to be "aware" that the patterns to which he was deeply socialized in the past are no longer operative in the present, and patterns to which he must become socialized in order to survive are, at times, barely emergent. Socialization to the past might result in death, imprisonment, even dishonor after the line changes. Too rapid socialization to the future might result in the same consequences, particularly if the individual is not able to predict the final line or future reversals, or the final level of stabilization of the line. At the same time the mechanical recitation of new or emerging formulae performed with the appearance of self-conscious knowledge would communicate to others that the individual in question is operating from perspectives other than the currently approved line. By suggesting such awareness, the individual conveys the image of an opportunist, a fence-sitter, or one who is not deeply committed to a line that in principle should be deeply internalized. Such a person communicates a lack of positive commitment to those who would judge his behavior on the basis of a commitment that is finalized only after the act of its communication. If one received and projected the right line too late, then an appearance of hesitancy, doubt, or of rational opportunism may make one subject to same kind of sanctions meted out to those who made the wrong choices.

Since changes in line, changes in personal loyalties, and the loosening and tightening of controls have occurred frequently in most societies described as totalitarian, the individual will have had the opportunity to observe the consequences of inappropriate behavior or lack of judgment. He will know the process, the cost, and the penalties and will have seen the consequences as they have operated on others, if not upon himself. He will have to have learned how to make the right decisions within the right time-frames, or else he may not be in a position to make those decisions. But, more important, he will have learned how to make those decisions without appearing to be the rational self-conscious decision-maker who has some other criteria (e.g., opportunism) for making the decision than those implied in ideology, the line, and the code. As an individual who has to make such life-maintaining decisions continuously, he must avoid developing or at least manifesting the self-consciousness and self-awareness that might make him his own most dangerous enemy. The private self of the decision-maker must be barred from self-consciousness. The only media available for making these decisions must be inaccessible to the self-conscious private self, but must operate as if the self-conscious self were totally rational. This is what George Orwell calls "doublethink," what Karl Mannheim pointed at in the concept of self-rationalization; it is Fromm's market personality, Riesman's "other-directedness," C. Wright Mill's self-salesmanship. But in all these "bourgeois" forms, the consequences of failure are not as great as in totalitarian societies, and therefore a higher degrees of consciousness of one's alienation are possible. Because the individual can be aware of the rational meaning of his deceitful speech and behavior he has time to learn the character-masks which permit his survival. In the process, he is able to feel the guilt and anxiety caused by his hypocrisy. Where these degrees of freedom are not allowed, where survival is totally dependent on the brainwashing of the self, one is not as likely to be conscious of one's alienation. One must develop deeper, less self-conscious commitments to those courses of action which permit survival. One cannot afford to be alienated.

In totalitarian societies and institutions, all of this takes place in social settings where one's behavior and speech are viewed by others who face the same ideological, political, and social imperatives. One may betray oneself, but one's betrayal may be to others whose own survival may require them to betray others in order to avoid betraying themselves. Thus, almost any other—friend, husband, wife, child, colleague, neighbor, or casual contact—can be an enemy. And this means that all actions and speech must be subject to the continuous regulation of the requirements of public "ideologies." This in turn means not the denial of privacy, but rather its intensification. The private sphere of the individual is so restricted that it is not even accessible to the self. It is ruled out of all social and business relations, and yet it remains hidden within the deep recesses of the human psyche. The fact that it remains can be demonstrated whenever, for some fortuitous reason, the line has changed, or when repression diminishes and some freedom is allowed; then individuals reveal access to thought, memories, and awareness that were banned at the time of the events reflected upon. The individual may not have been conscious of having such thoughts or awareness at the time the events occurred.

In another sense, the restrictions on privacy may be so severe that they constitute a deep internal pressure which demands release; yet the release would be destructive of the self. The problem of discovering how to release one's sense of an inner self, and how to communicate this sense, is of course a tremendous problem. In Soviet society—and many others—the problem is resolved in alcoholism. Drunkenness has been traditionally defined as an area where private behavior can be expressed outside of party lines. Thus, the drunken "brawl" becomes a social institution which has to be practiced assiduously to lighten the load of enforced privacy; the practice is frequent and repeated. In this sense alcoholism, especially as manifested in the Saturday night carouse, has, since the discovery of the distillation of spirits in the fourteenth century, been a standard response to dehumanization, whether inflicted by lords upon peasants, factory managers on wage workers, or commissars on everyone. In political totalitarianism, as in higher-level bureaucracies in capitalist society, there is a general understanding that people do not remember what they said "under the influence"; yet most manly participants to the orgy must know how "to drink like a man" and yet not say much that can be remembered on the following Sunday or Monday morning. At less extreme levels, a cultivation of personal friendship, of intimate social relations, becomes the object of special value; that is, the public, the political, the line, is barred from all personal and intimate relations, and in this abstraction of the private and intimate from the public, the hope is that relief from the public, the official, can be found in the purely personal. Personal charm, capacity for friendship, and mutual help at a private and intimate level become a special mystique in totalitarian societies, the object of envy for those who live in societies where the boundaries between public and the private are not so rigid.

Yet problems persist. When changes in the line are drastic, the inevitable self-revelation in one's personal and intimate relations can become the occasion for new persecution. In addition, the practice of public conformity combined with an emphasis on the intimate does not preclude normal career problems and desires. At critical periods in one's career, one may find it advantageous to achieve mobility or avoid pitfalls by throwing a friend to the wolves. The anxiety remains: What might I say now that five years from now, in a different ideological climate, line, or regime, can be used against me? This question must always be asked, and yet is frequently forgotten in those periods when the line is stable or when ideological purity is not being emphasized. In the periods when individuals are subject to denunciations, arrest, sanctions, and purges, the question must be asked: "What did I say to whom, how many years ago, that put me in this predicament?" Since the crimes for which one is subject to prosecution may be unimportant at the time of their commission, one may not remember them among the hundreds of thousands of acts and utterances one may casually make in a lifetime. When accused of an act, one may confess, but to the wrong crime, and so indict oneself through failure to remember what was not a crime at the time of commission.

With this as a background, the problem of who is a friend and who is an enemy, or rather, who is a potential friend and who a potential enemy, is a critical one. If one is unfortunate enough to have a consciousness of one's own separate identity along with a consciousness of the line and the consequences of following or not following it, then the problem becomes: "How, in my need to escape the inner burden of intellectual and political isolation, can I discover whom I can talk to?" Or "How can I communicate a sense of a desire to further open up to another that private vision which, if expressed to the wrong person, might be the source of my undoing?" Of course, the alcoholic party may provide, at gross levels, the possibility for the suspension of the rules maintaining personal and social distance. Vastly complicated speech and gestural patterns, which might imply an inner vision and a social existence apart from those embraced in a current line, may be projected in the hope that similar subtle responses may open up the possibility for less subtle, more intimate discussions and social interchanges. Yet, at the initial levels of such self-projections, language and actions must be so equivocal that, if the other does not wish to pursue them, one can withdraw even without communicating understanding. The gestures themselves must not be subject to immediate interpretation as contravening the line in its various manifestations. In such situations the achievement of intimacy may take place only over extended periods of time, but once achieved may be intensely valued. Betrayal in such situations provides an equally intense reaction since so much of one's self was invested in creating the social relation betrayed. In totalitarian situations, as well as in all situations where overcoming distance is hard, the scarcity value of friendship is extremely high, as are the recriminations at betrayal. In those societies, conversely, where it is easy to make friends it might be assumed that friendships are not deeply felt and are unable to withstand stresses that exceed the normal.

All of the dynamics described in the preceding pages, of course, operate in extreme situations or in those segments or levels of a totalitarian society where the pressures for conformity are greatest. We would expect these pressures, as in bureaucratic institutions, to be the highest at the middle and upper levels of the totalitarian society, with perhaps less freedom at the top than may exist in a bureaucratic society. One would expect the pressures to be greatest among intellectuals in a totalitarian society, where the attempt to achieve intellectual awareness involves a heightened self-consciousness which is likely to give itself away. It may also be greatest among those whose social position requires them to have opinions, and thus to be wrong if and when lines do change. Thus, totalitarian societies eat their children, those who make the revolution, defend it, and sustain it. The brutalized masses are protected by their ignorance, their lack of self-awareness, and their unimportance. In this sense, no totalitarian society can be fully totalitarian.

Privacy and Voluntary Associations

To the extent that individualism and privacy are a function of institutional pluralism, the possibility of their achievement necessarily rests on institutional development. The family and the locality originally serve as barriers to individualism, and the state and the economy provide for the emergence of alternatives. But both the state—i.e., the government—and the economic institutions can, as we have noted, become agents for the denial of individualism, as well as avenues for the expression of alternative aspects of the self. Another area of institutional development that allows for the creation of both public and intimate social roles is that of voluntary associations.

Voluntary associations have numerous origins. The first great secular voluntary association was the Masonic Orders. They were secular, being independent of and opposed to the church. They were also originally individualistic in their frequent opposition to the centralized state as that state began to emerge in the sixteenth and seventeenth centuries. They were political institutions demanding individual freedom and reforms. But they were also social organizations which gave expression to the instincts for sociability among autonomous free men. They developed a ritual that in part was a parody of the rituals of the upper classes, but in part that ritual was an expression of their commitment to a secular world of free men. They provided an area of freedom from the demands of the church, the state, and the business firm, to the extent that freemasonry was organized on the basis of individual qualification and membership. It must be recognized, however, that most Masons were drawn from the emerging business classes, along with dissident members of the aristocratic classes.

The double nature of voluntary associations is apparent in the fact that, while Masonry and all voluntary associations emphasize the freedom of their members from both narrower (the family) and wider (the state, the church, and the firm) institutions, they make demands for peer loyalties upon their members and subordinate them to a rich hierarchy of ritual and leadership within their own organizational sphere. But to the extent that that sphere is a relatively narrow one, constituting only one segment of the social life of the member, the subordination and commitment represent only a small segment of the total life and provide another set of alternatives to the members.

Masonry, even in its various subdivisions, was only the first of a wide variety of voluntary associations that arose, especially in the nineteenth century, to embrace the discretionary social life of the middle class in Western Europe and the United States. Many had other sources; some emerged out of the secularization of the Protestant sects, which themselves had stressed the autonomy of the congregation as distinct and separate from a hierarchy. The sects were self-selected organizations of peers who demanded from their potential members the highest standards of conduct as expressed in their Protestant origins. The obligation to the sect (and therefore one's peers) was superior to all other social obligations, though sect membership guaranteed the individual selected for membership access to social honor, to capital, to credit, and to markets. Thus membership in the sect was not inconsistent with economic individualism. But the sects denied privacy from the scrutiny of other sect members to the individual member. One's peers scrutinized the sect member's personal and private behavior, as well as his public behavior, to make sure that he was worthy of gaining and retaining membership in the sect. With the secularization of Protestantism in the nineteenth century, voluntary associations took over many of the functions of the sect. Initially they demanded exemplary conduct as a basis for membership. The voluntary character of membership and local basis of scrutiny by peers were "certificates of good character" that gave its members access to credit, markets, and clienteles. The religious tradition was continued in the sense that, regardless of the social amenities and ritual attached to the organization, each organization tended to have a civic and/or philanthropic purpose.

Most voluntary associations today retain such philanthropic purposes even though those purposes provide a minimum cover for the purely social activities that appear to constitute their central activities. Attendance at conventions, parties, organized sports, recreation, and simply having fun—these appear to be central. These latter activities appear to have grown precisely as the process of secularization increased, so that the philanthropic, religious, and civic functions of these secular organizations became even more secularized. By the 1920s it appeared that "pure sociability" was the main reason for existence of the voluntary associations; but again, this process is and was uneven. The voluntary associations in smaller towns were the last to abandon their original sect-derived functions. As sociability became more and more the primary, if not the exclusive, focus of the voluntary association, the ethical and moral imperatives diminished. In these new circumstances, the voluntary association became a shield, an area of "collective privacy" from the scrutiny of the communities of which they were a part. Membership was primarily confined to the middle and upper classes; the associations thus conferred status on those who had already achieved, or appeared to be in the position to achieve, social or economic status. Status *per se* became a replacement for moral and ethical behavior, as a requirement for membership. The semi-secret ritual and commitments of brotherhood allowed the membership to practice sociability and to have fun independently of the more backward Protestantism of the lower middle classes, who had not yet achieved the freedom from religion caused by an unevenly developing secularism. The clubhouse, the convention, and the meeting afforded an opportunity, during the era of Prohibition, to provide a place where illegal liquor could be drunk with impunity. The convention allowed for the exercise of sexual peccadilloes, with the recognition that fellow members were committed to honor the "privacy" of the individual, a privacy which was shared socially among the members but protected from the scrutiny of outsiders.

In the second half of the twentieth century, the country club, an autonomous organization not connected to a national body and having no philanthropic purpose, has replaced the voluntary association. Sports and recreation are its manifest purposes, but apart from that, in its socially organized discretion, it resembles the voluntary associations as they emerged in the first half of the century. In the latter half, the swinging singles apartment house provides a similar shielding of the deviant and a fairly public intimate life from the more official public morality and scrutiny of the society at large.

We are less concerned with the so-called immorality of the modern voluntary association than with the fact that they have increasingly provided a social screen for a collective privacy and are institutions where the normally constituted social constraints are suspended, where the individual can act socially as if he were a private person. Secularization in the voluntary association and the club becomes a way for privacy to be an attribute no longer of an individual but of a social circle. The members are collectively private against the public demands of outsiders.

Notes

1. Flanders Dunbar, *Mind and Body: Psychosomatic Medicine* (New York: Random House, 1947), pp. 45, 51, 157–163, *et passim*. Also John C. Nemiah, "The Concept of Psychosomatic Medicine" (chapter XVIII), in *Foundations of Psychopathology* (New York: Jason Aronson, 1973).

2. Erving Goffman, *Stigma: Notes on the Management of Spoiled Identity* (Englewood Cliffs, N.J.: Prentice-Hall, 1963), discusses many such conditions and offers a rich bibliography.

3. Goffman, *Stigma*, p. 127.

4. Evelyn Hooker, "The Homosexual Community," in Palmer and Goldstein, ed., *Perspectives in Psychopathology: Readings in Abnormal Psychology* (New York: Oxford University Press, 1966). Also Dorothy J. Douglas, "Managing Fronts in Observing Deviance," in Jack Douglas, ed., *Research on Deviance* (New York: Random House, 1972).

5. August Aichhorn, *Wayward Youth: A Psychoanalytic Study of Delinquent Children,* foreword by S. Freud (New York: Viking Press, 1935; Meridian Books reprint, 1960).

6. Edward Sagarin, "Survival Patterns and Social Control" (chapter V), in *Deviants and Deviance: An Introduction to the Study of Disvalued People and Behavior* (New York: Praeger, 1975), especially the sections "Strategies of the Deviants," "Dissembling and Dissimulation," and "Normals Against Deviants."

7. Joseph Bensman and Robert Lilienfeld, "The Psychologist" (chapter 10), in *Craft and Consciousness: Occupational Technique and the Development of World Images* (New York: John Wiley, 1973), esp. pp. 176–179.

8. S. Freud, *New Introductory Lectures on Psychoanalysis,* trans. and ed. James Strachey (New York: Norton, 1964), 72–74. "The id of course knows no judgments of value: no good and evil, no morality. The economic or, if you prefer, the quantitative factor, which is intimately linked to the pleasure principle, dominates all of its processes. Institutional cathexes seeking discharge—that, in our view, is all there is in the id" (p. 74).

See also Charles Brenner, "The Drives" (chapter 2), in *An Elementary Textbook of Psychoanalysis* (Garden City, N.Y.: Anchor Books, 1957).

9. Andrew Crowcroft, *The Psychotic: Understanding Madness* (Baltimore: Penguin Books, 1967), and John C. Nemiah, *Foundations of Psychopathology* (New York: Jason Aronson, 1973).

10. Two plays by Henrik Ibsen especially illuminate the construction by individuals of delusional systems and their trapping of their close intimates in these delusions: *John Gabriel Borkman* and *The Master Builder.*

11. Erving Goffman, *Frame Analysis: An Essay on the Organization of Experience* (New York: Harper & Row, 1974), p. 462, relates a similar incident. The entire essay contains material relevant to this discussion.

12. W. J. H. Sprott, "Experimental Groups: Working Together" (chapter 7), in *Human Groups* (Baltimore: Penguin Books, 1958).

13. Czeslaw Milosz, *The Captive Mind,* trans. Jane Zielonko (New York: Random House, 1951).

14. Erving Goffman, *Asylums* (Garden City, N.Y.: Anchor Books, 1961); Rosabeth Moss Kanter, *Commitment and Community* (Cambridge, Mass.: Harvard University Press, 1972).

15. The literature here is very large. A few titles deserve special mention: George Orwell, *1984*; Alexander Solzhenitsyn, *The First Circle*; Leopold Tyrmand: *The Rosa Luxemburg Contraceptives Cooperative: A Primer on Communist Civilization* (New York: Macmillan, 1972); Nadezhda Mandelstam, *Hope against Hope: A Memoir*, trans. Max Hayward (New York: Atheneum, 1970, and *Hope Abandoned*, trans. Max Hayward (New York: Atheneum, 1974).

Chapter 4

Intimacy

The private world of the person inevitably conflicts with the public world of culture and society. If we surrender to the public world, we become other-oriented, market personalities or, if living in societies where individuation has never been achieved, we simply do not exist as individuals. But the burden of being an individual, of resisting the absorption of our personality by social groups or by an "objective" culture, is great. We have seen that psychosis is a form of compulsive privacy, one of the many forms of privacy that is less than the realization of the whole individual, a defense against the trauma of being overwhelmed by group or community standards.

Max Weber has indicated that it is almost impossible for individuals to stand up against the objectivity of the totality of culture. The range of cultural values presented to one as a totality is impossible to assimilate, especially when that range is replete with contradictions between the various cultural values. Each value presents itself as a god, and each value makes absolute demands upon the individual for attention and loyalty. Each demand is presented in rational, logical form, while the conflict of those values gives the individual who internalizes more than one value both the appearance and the reality of operating with totally contradictory and irrational bases for action and decision. The results, according to Weber, are the cultivation of the irrational and, often, of the private. The individual ignores the demands of an objective range of culture. He makes arbitrary choices, most often on emotional grounds. But in addition, in extreme situations he withdraws to intimate and quasi-public groups created for the purpose of withdrawal from a public, official life whose tenets, if taken seriously, would be impossible to accept. The cult, the sect, and the community of charismatic followers are such quasi-public groups.[1]

We would add this to Weber's analysis: The intimate and the quasi-public are not creations that emerge in extreme situations. They are always with us in continuously changing forms and with ever changing labels.

The family, the neighborhood, the cult, and the sodality, the primitive *Gemeinde,* are ancient forms that precede the creation of rational, objective, public culture in the sense we have defined the public. They persist or, in the case of the charismatic community, reappear in crises of objective culture. The quasi-public reemerges as the "gang"; the peer group as the "informal" organization, the friendship, the sorority, fraternity, club, salon, social circle, the *cortegiano,* and we rediscover it, in this book, as the social network, the intimate, and the quasi-public. In societies that are not primitive, where the public and the private have separated, the private becomes in part a reaction to the public, to the fact that much of the biological impulses and "reaction formations" of the individual cannot be expressed in public. But the totally private, in its opposition to the overwhelming weight of public culture, is also intolerable. The intimate, in all its various social forms, becomes a means of socializing the private, of giving social support and expression to the private. When such social support becomes recognized in social relations that extend beyond two persons, beyond the purely intimate, we call the resulting form of social relationship and its culture the *quasi-public.*

Intimacy and Privacy

We have indicated that peer group formations tend to arise out of the attempt to resist the pressures from agents of the public world—parents, teachers, officials. Peer groups also emerge among mobile aspirants to the public world when their aspirations are not yet achieved, as an uneasy alliance of those bent on "making it."

They emerge among deviants who attempt to find social space within which the recognition and practice of their deviancy is not viewed as stigma and not subject to social sanctions. And finally, they emerge as cliques, personal friendship groups in large-scale organizations, which in principle deny friendship as a basis for official business.[2]

Intimacy is a safety-valve for the self. But there are many kinds of intimacy. Some kinds are imposed upon individuals by the very structure of social life—a kind of intimacy that individuals may not want and may resist but for which they have little choice. The prison, the army barracks, the hospital ward, and the dormitory are large-scale administrative organizations which rearrange the life of the individual so that privacy is not possible. At the same time those aspects of the life functions of the individuals usually considered private are subject to public view and comment by one's enforced peers. In such cases one has the "socialization" of the private; the underside of the personality is made public, and the "objective culture" of the barracks is the private. Individuals who value privacy, who value their sense of self, find the public exposure of the barracks intolerable. Moreover, the culture of the barracks is crude, vulgar, obscene. That which is normally hidden goes on public display and is the object of derision, assault, buffoonery, and sadism. Within barracks life almost no other form of expression is possible. Thus a major theme in all literature is the humiliation of the sensitive individual in the vulgarity of the military, the prison, the hospital. The intimacy of the barracks is not based on the voluntary exchange of personal confidences, of trust, of affection and warmth. It might, in modern society, be considered a form of pseudo-intimacy.[3]

We indicated in Chapter 1 that some kinds of primitive society, because of the smallness of the groups involved and the confinement in relatively tight spatial areas, make the achievement of privacy almost impossible. In addition, achievement of some degree of intimacy with particular others may be seen as a threat to the group, a conspiracy, sorcery, the practice of witchcraft. Yet it would be hard to see in such situations the denial of privacy, because we have indicated that a high valuation placed on privacy is a cultural phenomenon, the result of long periods of cultural and intellectual growth, and becomes a norm relatively late in the history of mankind. The enforced intimacy in primitive societies need not be experienced as a denial of the individual, because in such societies the individual cannot properly be said to exist. In such situations, the denial of privacy and of intimacy need not be experienced as denial.

This position can be overstated. In some primitive societies, public ritual and ceremony may be so highly developed, so much a part of the tradition, that the public ceremony, the public *per se*; is overwhelming, and the individual may withdraw to nonceremonial, nontraditional activities, often called "the profane." Some level of privacy and intimacy may be permitted until it is viewed as threatening to the group. Yet the individualism, the privacy, the intimacy so permitted tends to be devalued and secondary. Such individualism ultimately became the media out of which genuine ideologies of privacy, of concepts of self, have emerged historically, primarily in religion.

The development of most great world religions has tended to emerge in the cultivation of the private, the relationship of the individual to a god in opposition to the primitive conception that a god is or should be the protector and the ancestor of the object of worship of the community, a clan, or a kinship group.

Pseudo-Intimacy

The emergence of the private and its support for the intimate took thousands of years in arriving, and it has never fully arrived. That is, religions that value the private inevitably become organized as social groups, and the struggle to establish the religion as an acceptable or dominant organization and to establish the legitimacy of its message, forces religious leaders ultimately to exercise discipline over its membership. Religious reinstitute public codes, which individuals in their quest for a sense of self resist by retreating to the private and the intimate.

In primitive worlds, restrictions on social space force the individual to live in a world where what is usually considered the private and the intimate is continually the object of public observation. Poverty also devalues privacy. The achievement of privacy requires physical space, and everywhere poverty forces individuals to live in constricted space. The behavior that is private, insofar as it reflects the biological, the perverse, the unsocialized, is forced into the open, because the open exists by virtue of the fact that space is restricted and there is no place for the private. The pseudo-intimacy of poverty denies the genuine intimacy based on the possibility of the achievement of privacy. The possibility of sublimating biological behavior is thus denied, and crudity and vulgarity become a norm imposed upon the poor by the lack of opportunity for privacy. At the same time, poverty denies the poor the opportunity to achieve the cultural resources necessary to stylize their private taste and their intimate thoughts. The poverty of the relatively isolated rural poor can at times provide the space that allows the yeoman to develop some measure of personal dignity and sense of self, a dignity that urban intellectuals often envy and idealize.[4] Urban sophisticates will often envy the healthy extroversion, the vulgar good humor, and the insensitivity of the poor, since it seems to them that the poor are not burdened with neuroticism, introversion, and anxiety—all products of an overdeveloped sense of self that is part of the burden of privacy.

Another form of pseudo-intimacy is that of the Mardi Gras, the brawl, or the stag party. Individuals overburdened by the rigidity of social codes, which in the normal course of events seems to them to deny their biological humanity and to place them under overwhelming constraints, desire to suspend the rigid rules—as do the perverted —in organized clubs, events, and special occasions. The alumni party and the Legion convention become opportunities for individuals who are not intimate in ordinary situations to agree implicitly that their lack of intimacy will not be held against them when they act as biological individuals or as deviants, or act in terms of their own private normal standards. They can act as if they were "perverted." The pseudo-intimacy of suspended social rules acts perhaps as a safety valve for those who are subject to stringent moral and behavioral codes but who have not been deeply socialized to those codes. In such situations, people apparently subdued and decorous in behavior, proper, and even righteous reveal both the power of public norms in governing public occasions and the failure of those norms to operate at deep psychological levels. They also reveal the difficulties of achieving the deep internalization of public norms. When rule-suspending organizations become part of the normal social organization of a community, and when the members of them meet routinely, they contribute to a schizophrenic community. One set of rules involves the development of secrecy about the activities in the rule-suspending organization. The country club, the civic association, the weekly poker game, and the hunting party all require the "proper" members of the communities who participate not to reveal the activities in which they participate. The private or the intimate expressed in these rule-suspending organizations violates the public behavior of the community as recognized in community-wide norms. The intimacy revealed in such organizations has similar characteristics to that concealed by the secrecy of the perverted. Yet again, one must add that such secrecy is part of the safety valve of living, in one's public behavior, a publicly proper life. Scandal in such communities is usually based on the disclosure of the private behavior practiced in intimate groups that violate publicly-upheld norms. Hypocrisy on a community-wide basis is the price a community pays for maintaining both the public norms and the private intimate worlds which deny those norms.

For those who must live their life in public and must accede to public norms, the maintenance of rule-suspending organizations becomes an economically affordable necessity if they hope to maintain private and intimate behavior that violates these norms. The affordable is the product of wealth, affluence, and social position, all of which makes the maintenance of public norms both necessary and possible. The affluent can therefore get away with behavior that the less affluent cannot practice with impunity.

The existence of rule-suspending events and organizations is a product of affluence. But, since only the affluent can enjoy both the rewards of public position and respectability and the vices denied by those positions, they are resented by others for being able to practice without stigma that behavior for which the poor are stigmatized. Such resentment becomes a social reality, and it takes the form of the invasion of privacy. The mass media, since their very inception, have profited by the public disclosure of the private behavior by the rich, the powerful, and the righteous that denies public morality. In doing so, the media have continuously made what had been the private or intimate into public property. Today not only are we increasingly aware of dereliction of public duty by our presidents, but we are told also of their sexual impotence or priapism, their long-term affairs, and their cafeteria sexuality. We are informed, whether we wish to be or not, of the alcoholism of their wives, their compulsive consumerism, their petty greed, and their theft of the public treasury. To some extent, great leaders will cater to this quest for scandal by defining it as "humanity."[5] President Johnson will reveal the scars on his belly, and candidate Carter his intellectual "lust," as calculated devices to prove they have a private human self. President Nixon maintained a sharp separation between the public and the private—in public being a sanctimonious upholder of Protestant morality, and in private an unimaginative exponent of linguistic obscenity. We can never be sure that the private obscenity of Richard Nixon was kept private in order to make a public profit at some later date (from his memoirs), a date which was moved forward under court order. President Johnson, who was reputedly a far greater master of invective and obscenity, managed to maintain the separation between the public and the private with respect to his speech, but not his navel. The quest for revelation of the obscenely private has become a compulsive drive in the second half of the twentieth century. It does not suggest the humanity of the public official, the star, or the celebrity, but rather his degradation. But more important, it suggests that the boundaries between the public and the private begin to dissolve; it is no longer as necessary to maintain a sense of a separate self, as was the case in the not too distant past. It becomes more difficult to maintain a sense of the self based on distinctively private and individual behavior; if this happens to our most distinguished leaders, it means that we are not obliged to act as individuals. Confession becomes a public form of self-presentation.

The invasion of privacy is not only a function of the mass media; it is also a function of the mass organization. With the development of large-scale bureaucracies comes the development of professionally organized security services, whether it be the CIA, the FBI, private detective and security services, and consultants and certifiers of the public and private purity of would-be applicants and candidates for promotions, as well as certifiers of the immorality and criminality of rivals, opposing candidates, and competitors. The high point of all this, perhaps, might have been J. Edgar Hoover's surveillance of the sexual lives of Martin Luther King, congressmen who passed on FBI budgets, and even his superiors, including the President. The motives appear to be mixed; certainly Hoover enjoyed the voyeurism of the bedroom tape, and he apparently enjoyed the sharing of choice tidbits with President Kennedy.[6] Both as bureaucratic empire-builder and as a law-enforcement officer, he enjoyed the invasion of privacy as perhaps private illegal extension of his manifest public duties.

The mass media devalue privacy as part of their public profit-making enterprise, by feeding the resentment of those who apparently cannot enjoy vice to the same extent as do their superiors. Large-scale organizations tend to invade privacy, in large part, in order to use the information so gained as a private means to secure its public goals and in part by using managed leaks to reveal the private vices of their organizational and personal enemies. In both cases they devalue the qualities of privacy itself, and thus devalue, by the inflation of exposure, the power of the means they use. The net result is only the devaluation of privacy.

Prostitution as Pseudo-Intimacy

Another form of pseudo-intimacy can be found in prostitution. A full discussion of prostitution would require a resumption of our discussion of biological and sexual privacy. We have noted that the biological systems become invested with meanings that go far beyond the biological. We indicated that blows to the sense of self become translated into disturbances in the cardiovascular, respiratory, and digestive systems. The same applies to the sexual system. We have also noted that such disturbances in the sexual system have been given special emphasis in psychology despite the fact that the latter are usually not as physically dangerous as the former. Thus, the sexual functioning of the individual undoubtedly more deeply embodies the sense of self than do the other physiological systems. Perhaps the reason why sex may be symbolically more important than breathing is that sex is not only an expression of the private but also an expression of the intimate. Except for auto-eroticism, sex, while embodying the biological individual, is a social act (and auto-eroticism is usually accompanied by social-sexual fantasy), and it is an act that at the physiological level implies the greatest closeness possible. The terms "penetration," or "skin-to-skin" reflect this degree of closeness, as, at the physiological level, the term "knowing" reflects a deeper level of closeness. Sexual partners appear to know each other not necessarily more deeply but rather more closely than they know each other at other levels. Again, at the physiological level, that closeness may be mutual. Thus, a mother caring for a child may know the child deeply and totally at the child's physiological level, but that relationship is not necessarily symmetrical. The nurse or doctor or ward attendant may know a patient at deep physiological levels, but again the relationship is not symmetrical. At least formally, the sexual relationship is close and symmetrical. Some Freudians, especially Freud, Fromm, and Otto Pollak, have argued that the heterosexual relationship is not symmetrical, because women, having internal sex organs and internal orgasms, are able to conceal their sexual response far more than can men, and these differences account for a large part of the psychology of women. Women can fake orgasm and men cannot; since man's failure is more evident than that of a woman, women can use their relative invulnerability to criticism to attack the more manifest inadequacies of men. On these grounds, Freudians argue that women are more secretive than men, psychologically inclined to greater "privacy" in their deviancy. Men, reflecting their sexual "openness," are more aggressive and overt in their deviancy.[7]

We doubt the universality of the application of these physiological differences, simply because varieties in sexual practice allow for the overcoming of these differences.

Physiological and Psychological Intimacy

If the act of sex is an expression of both the private and the intimate, one cannot conclude that the sexual act *per se* is an intimate act. It may be a pseudo-intimate act. That is, a single sexual act with a stranger, as in prostitution or casual promiscuity, involves a minimal penetration of selves, a minimum sense of intimacy, even though the physiological act appears to be intimate. Thus, it is necessary to distinguish between physiological and psychological intimacy. Physiological intimacy implies only closeness, the penetration of bodies but nothing more. Psychological intimacy implies the interpenetration of selves, of personalities.

But the fact that, in sexual relations, the two forms of intimacy are so closely related makes it possible to confuse the two. Physiological intimacy may become a symbol of or substitute for psychological intimacy. The desperately lonely, the personally repressed, the isolated, or the unappreciated may use casual sex or prostitution as a means of overcoming deeper psychological needs for intimacy. Of course, such sexuality is usually unsatisfying, though at times it may provide a momentary physiological release for sexual tension, whether that tension be sexual in origin or a displaced need for human contact at deeper psychological levels. The need for social contact may be compulsive, and sexual contact, being a mode of expressing the self in social situations, becomes more compulsive than the sexual need as a physiological need.

As a result of the poverty of physiological sex as a means of expressing the self, casual sexuality is generally considered unsatisfactory and of momentary importance. As a result, it frequently may be used as a means of degrading the self, punishing oneself for having failed to achieve satisfactory social relations in other spheres of life. Most of the literature on prostitution suggests that the psychological motive for entering prostitution is the same need to humiliate the self. The same general diagnosis applies to promiscuity and Don Juanism. However, one cannot generalize this hypothesis; perhaps far more important is simply the fact of failure. The quest for physiological sexual intimacy is a product of the failure to achieve intimacy at other levels, including genuine sexual intimacy.

Prostitution and casual sexuality—the intimacy between strangers —offer an intimacy that does not achieve the gratification of psychological intimacy, primarily because it is based on the single sex act. In that act some parts of the deeper self are projected, but those projected aspects are minimal. Repeated sexual activity with the same partner over extended periods of time necessarily involves a greater exchange, a greater surrender, of knowledge of the other, and a greater possibility that such knowledge will be symmetrical. The individual reveals more of what is private to himself, more of his weaknesses, of what is usually hidden, more of what he consciously conceals from strangers. The individual may attempt, even in repeated sexual unions, to conceal those aspects of the self which he regards as humiliating, deviant, or self-revealing. Yet repeated contact at even the physiological level makes this difficult. The individual reveals more in such cases than he may want to. Prostitution and other forms of sexual behavior that are defined socially as "perverse," however, allow for a peculiar kind of self-revelation. The individual, in such situations, is allowed to reveal deviant and perverse aspects of his behavior, but he is usually not allowed to reveal that which is "normal." Thus, prostitution and other forms of "perverted" or "deviant" behavior allow for an inverted revelation of the self, primarily those parts which are denied in normal social intercourse. At the same time, such self-revelation is usually not symmetrical. The prostitute is often required to bolster the ego of her client by faking love or sexual response and to humiliate herself by providing her client with a life history leading to her course of deviance, the origins of her fall from grace, in order to entertain her client's prurience. She is paid to maintain the ego of her client at the expense of her own. As a professional, she may accept the task by providing a stylized fictional biography and the appearance of love, while maintaining her distance from her client. Fiction is thus used by the prostitute as a means of defending her genuine privacy and her intimate but wounded self, even in the intimacy of the sexual act. If the prostitute were to demand a symmetrical relationship, requiring the same kinds of self-revelation from her client that she fictionally provides to him, she would be treating her client as an equal, and in doing so she would be degrading him to a level to which the client normally is unwilling to descend. From the standpoint of the client, the intimacy that he demands of the prostitute is not an intimacy that he willingly grants. In not granting the equality of intimacy, he treats the intimacy of sex as a limited intimacy, a purely physiological intimacy, and not a psychological one.

In continuous repeated sexual contact the artificial barriers to intimacy are harder to maintain. They can more easily spill over into psychological intimacy. Thus the individual, wittingly or unwittingly, reveals more of his/her self, reveals aspects of the self that he is unlikely to reveal in other social relations. He reveals weaknesses, vulnerabilities, vanities, and psychological damage at far deeper and more subtle levels than he might unwittingly reach even in perverse forms of casual prostitution. As one begins to reveal the totality of the self, one becomes more truly human.

Of course this is rarely achieved to the fullest degree. The upper-class, educated, more subtle, finer-grained partner in an extended sexual liaison or marriage, because of class superiority or vanity, or out of defense of unappreciated characteristics and traits, may choose to withhold, even over a lifetime, aspects of the self that he regards as likely to be trampled on if revealed. And of course, we must hasten to add that not all individuals know themselves to the extent that they can consciously reveal themselves. They conceal parts of their total personalities from themselves and, in doing so, necessarily conceal those aspects of the self from even the most intimate others. At the same time, they may unwittingly reveal more of the self than they intend to. And the intimate other, realizing that part of the revealed attitude is unknown or denied to the self, may be forced to withhold his or her knowledge of the other. Thus, the act of aggression in marital and sexual conflict among sexual intimates may consist in revealing to the other those aspects of the other which the other may be consciously or unconsciously attempting to deny. In exposing the other to himself, the intimate aggressor may consciously or unconsciously be attempting to destroy that arrangement of the self of the other that is the basis of the other's total personality. At this point, the frank exchange of knowledge of the self and the other may be total warfare, aimed—again consciously or unconsciously—at destroying the other. Intimacy, at its deepest, most frank level, thus is not necessarily supportive of ongoing social relations. Intimacy requires tact, compassion, love, charity, and, above all, trust.

The Intimacy of Marriage

The intimacy of marriage, of deep and enduring sexual relations, is such that within the course of the relationship each party cannot help but reveal to the other the whole range of biological, physical, and social infirmities that are part of the human condition. Certainly, sex provides the basis for a part of this self-revelation, but much more is involved. Within the kinds of relaxation of the censoring self, the parties reveal such infirmities as greed, vanity, sadism, pettiness, tendencies toward dishonesty, and forms of neurosis and near-psychosis, which may appear either as part of a basic character structure or as forms that emerge episodically in the flow of a continuous and enduring relationship. Even less "psychological" manifestations of the personality are revealed more sharply to the intimate other. Bad habits, personal dirtiness, drunkenness, or obscenity of speech, either in intimate circles or under the influence of alcohol, are revealed, where in less intimate situations the same habits may be concealed. The injunction to care for one another causes each party to see elements of dependency that are characteristic of an infant. A husband may vomit, and a wife may have to clean up both the mess and the husband. Diarrhea may cause the partner of the weakened person to be responsible for the other's filth. The partner who is strong on the occasion of the other's weakness has to repress his/her fastidiousness, distaste, or horror in order to look after the other. The continuous collective social interaction between the pair and outsiders makes each party aware of the censored self-projections that each party presents to outsiders. One partner cannot help but witness the lies, white or black, that the other party tells, knowing from his or her previous observation that the lie is a lie, and deliberately so. One witnesses the preparations for the masquerades of social snobbery, deception, and manipulation of outsiders. And to the extent that the marital couple is a team, each partner is forced, at least in public, to support the lies and pretensions, the masquerades, the censored behavior and language, of the other. To tell the truth in the face of one's partner's lies is to attack the ego of the partner and to invite a public brawl.

The Social Requirements of Intimacy

Some "foreign relations" of the marital pair are based on shared understandings as to the nature of the public presentation that they as a family will project. The myth they attempt to create is the creation of both parties, and because their myth is a collective effort neither party needs to make explicit the truth, which must be distorted in order to make that public presentation. The social myth is based on unstated assumptions and has behind it the total strength of their collective effort.

In other cases the mobile family, especially the snobbish family, may be highly organized to plan long-term campaigns to reach the goals of their collective enterprise. In other cases, one party may feel the pressure for a favorable self-presentation as being his or her primary function; the other may be forced merely to provide support, confirmation, and, minimally, the absence of denial. In such cases the supporting person is likely to be consciously aware of the deception practiced on outsiders by the partner but must be tolerant, at least in public, of that deception. Certainly, if the deceptive practice represents a basic personality characteristic of a partner, reminding the partner of the weakness or deception represents a total strain on the entire relationship. Tolerance, turning a blind eye, is thus a basic requirement of intimacy, even if intimacy is defined as a pragmatic necessity of the social relationship. But in these situations, where the managed social deception is an intrinsic part of the social relationship, each party to the relationship will, over the course of time, have plenty of opportunity to see his or her partner caught in the act of social deception, humiliated, and defeated. If there is some degree of hostility between the two, each may partially enjoy the defeat of the other. But if he/she enjoys the defeat too openly or reminds the other of past humiliations, he/she threatens the social relationship. More important, because in the normal course of an enduring marital relationship such humiliations and defeats inevitably occur, and occur within the purview of the partner, toleration, support, and aid in overcoming the sense of defeat are all necessities of an intimate social relationship. Frequently the parties will witness, in the behavior of the intimate other, behavior that would be intolerable if practiced by a stranger. The witnessing other must suspend his/her generalized standards of behavior when applied to the intimate other, or he/she risks disruption of the social relationship.

The Symmetry of Flawed Humanity

In all of these illustrations, we have pointed to the fact that one party in the intimate relationship is in a position of observing the flawed humanity of the other. Of course, social relations are far more complex; each party in a symmetrical social relationship will be able to see the flaws of the other, and each will be required to exercise minimally a level of tolerance in order to maintain the relationship. The minimal level of tolerance is the pragmatic price one pays for intimacy. If only one person is flawed or only one person reveals his/her flaws, the relationship develops asymmetry. Needless to say, partners may be chosen for their potential asymmetry in the relationship. One partner can use his or her concealment, or his or her righteousness, as a device for dominating the other. Such a relationship is likely to endure only if the flawed person has a need for being dominated or cannot escape domination, that is, needs to return to a condition of infantile dependency or is unable to leave it. Conversely, the need to conceal one's flawed humanity from an intimate other may well be a device to perpetuate one's dominance over an apparent equal.

We have said that a minimal level of tolerance is the pragmatic minimal basis for an enduring intimate relationship. Such a viewpoint may be cynical, yet we have specified that this pragmatic tolerance is only the minimal precondition of an intimate social contract. Obviously, most situations of intimacy are based on more than these minimal preconditions. Thus, genuine love, affection, a sense of a shared fate or destiny, personal attraction, and common interests and culture all make tolerance of a flawed humanity more than mere tolerance. At the same time, one must insist that flawed humanity is not an exception to the condition of man. The flaws are "flaws" only because social and cultural values select and reward only some aspects of character and behavior, and other aspects are devalued, at least in their public performance.

Tolerance based on love and affection consists of overlooking behavior and characteristics that would be devalued if exhibited in public by a stranger, or else it consists in excusing or "understanding" such behavior. Empathy in such situations means the recognition that the corresponding flaws of the other, when practiced in either public or intimate situations, are the flaws that one is oneself capable of exhibiting in public, private, or intimate behavior. Thus one suspends judgment—and develops particularity in patterns of judgment—on the basis of empathy. In these terms a universalistic suspension of judgment would be the denial of all public life; that is, there would be no standards of behavior to which an individual as citizen or as public actor would be accountable. That is, the suspension of standards of judgment or the toleration of otherwise unacceptable characteristics and behavior is based on the notion that there are public standards of behavior to which individuals in general, particularly loved ones, can be held accountable. Without such "universal" standards of behavior, society would not be possible; everything would be permissible, and no holds would be barred. Without universal standards of behavior (abeit particular to a given time, place, and social milieu), no particular society or culture would be possible. All this means only that society exists on the basis of its standards and values, its rules and laws. And yet intimacy is based upon and results in the suspension of these standards, because of a pragmatic desire for such a mutual suspension in order to escape their stringencies or out of genuine love and affection. As a result, there is a basic conflict between the intimate group and the society, or the larger, more publicly organized groups.

Universalistic Social Standards and Particularistic Intimate Ones

Intimate groups exist to contravene the general social norms or, conversely, to escape the more universalistic demands of larger groups. They provide relief from the stringency of universalistic demands, but in doing so they threaten the universalistic standards of such larger groups. This tension is intrinsic to the operation of all societies. The more "the society" insists on universalistic demands, the more it denies the particularism of private experience and creates the need for intimate groups within which the universalistically denied can be particularistically expressed. The alternative "social strategy" produces corresponding problems: The more the society develops tolerance, the less it can insist, by definition, on the standards that determine its particular form of universalism, and the more it is likely to permit those forms of asocial, antisocial, and reactive behavior which deny the existence of any organized society. The contradiction between the insistence on universalistic standards and the release of socially and psychologically repressed biological and reactive deviant behavior is intrinsic to the very operation of society. So far as we know, there is no *a priori* balance point that automatically resolves the problem. Societies will oscillate between overrepression and extreme permissiveness; each extreme will tend to reveal the flaws in its respective "solution" to the problem. And in reacting, either to overrepression or to overpermissiveness, it will tend to produce its opposite. This too could be called a "dialectic of history"; insofar as we know, it is a dialectic without end. But like all other dialectics it cannot be resolved, as we apparently have done, by a neat use of the word *dialectic,* for the forms of societal repression are unique in each historical and cultural epoch and are given definition only by the continuous evolution of culture, values, and religion. The forms of permissiveness extant are given definition by the sense of repression predominantly experienced in the previous era. The forms of permissiveness and the demand for permissiveness are products of, among other things, the particular forms of repression experienced in the immediate past.

Moreover, the articulation of new demands both for freedom and for law and order is the product of historically unique and at best partially autonomous intellectual, religious, and cultural articulation and is never predictable on any *a priori* basis. If there is oscillation between the forms of permissiveness and repression, the oscillations are not predictable within any given time period, despite—we would argue—numerous attempts to find a periodic flow of culture.

And finally, to repeat ourselves, these oscillations are not the departure and return from given forms of permissiveness or repression, but rather are to ever new but renewed forms and styles of opposition and return.

Love and Tolerance

Let us return to a more intimate level of discussion. We have indicated that empathy, tolerance, and the suspension of criticism for violations of publicly proclaimed values and standards are essential ingredients and values within intimate relations. The mediating emotions in all but the minimal formal social contract are love and affection. This has additional consequences: The most immediate cause of the disruption of intimate social relations is most likely to be the withdrawal of love or affection. That is to say, changes in behavior between two or more parties to an intimate relationship are less likely to cause a disruption in the behavior than do changes in the affectional relationship that result in the withdrawal of the suspension of criticism or of the tolerance of previously acceptable behavior.

One event may result in such a suspension of tolerance, may cause the individual to open one's eyes, to see what one hasn't seen before or to see meanings to behavior which one hasn't recognized before, or to find that a given patterns of behavior of another is no longer tolerable. Thus, in asymmetrical relationships, the growth of health and self-confidence or the availability of desirable alternatives may cause one party to see that the behavior of the other, which was tolerable for much of a lifetime, is no longer tolerable. That party may break up the relationship, entering into new relationships with others who at different levels necessarily demand other kinds of affectually given suspensions of criticism or intolerance.

Of course, not all disruptions of intimate relationships are based on the suspension of intolerance. Certainly, very few social relationships are based on the reproduction of exact forms of other-oriented behavior. The very operation of the life cycle itself, as well as one's relations with outsiders to an intimate relationship, alters the actions that become part of the intimate relationship, and these may strain the levels of tolerance or suspension of criticism within that relationship. Given these vicissitudes of normal life, it is far more remarkable that intimate social relationships persist over extended periods of time, including the lifetime of individuals. Affection and love must then be conceived as enormously important as deep and pervasive constituents of human life, far more than a formally cynical outlook would lead us to expect. At the same time, the persistence of intimate social relations through extended periods of life attests to the failure of public norms, of standardized culture and social rules, to allow for the full expression of the total selves that make up an individual.

Society as an Enemy of the "Private" and the "Intimate"

The fact that "society" imposes rules and denies the full expression of the total individual is, and has been, a prominent source of discontent in all advanced worlds. In the modern Western world, *Don Quixote* is perhaps the first document to the tyranny of the social over the individual. But, like virtually all such protests, the protest is against a particular form of the social; for Cervantes it was the meanness, the pettiness, the prosaic and unimaginative materialism in Don Quixote's immediate world that caused him to escape into a world of dreams and delusions, which were far more idealistic and eloquent than the petty world of the present.

Certainly, since the rise of the novel, one principal theme has been the assault on the private individual by the organized social repression of the bourgeoisie, the upper classes, and, as external circumstances have changed, an aristocracy or fascist and communist elites. Yet one must hasten to add that it is not political repression that is the central focus of most novels. With respect to the rise of the bourgeoisie the sources of repression were shallow materialism, philistinism, lack of sensitivity, lack of culture, and submission to sterile parochial social norms. Novels depicting the upper classes tend to focus on the offhand dismissal by the upper classes of culti-vated but naive *arrivistes* and on the violation of upper-class stand-ards by the upper class, along with their violation of the standards of the bourgeoisie. The short-lived antifascist and anti-Nazi novel—short-lived because of the short lives of the regimes that were its setting—focused on brutality, hypocrisy, and the denial of life in their full range in these regimes. They also focused on the opportun-ism, the shallowness, and, within the private sphere, the degeneracy of the fascist's life. Certainly the anticommunist novel is no different from the antifascist novel, except that it depicts a more pervasive brutality practiced far more hypocritically under the guise of com-munist universalism.

Yet it is the antibourgeois novel which emphasized intimacy as a value against the hypocrisy and sterility of bourgeois and upper-middle-class life. D. H. Lawrence concentrated on the free, untram-meled expression of sexuality as the life-giving and life-expressing part of the individual.

And it is Lawrence, perhaps more than Cervantes or Kafka, or Solzhenitsyn or Thomas Mann, who in the novel captures the sense of the failure of individuals to achieve genuine intimacy. Certainly, the Lawrentian themes pervade a vast number of novels and mass culture, even to the present. But more than that, they capture the struggle of men and women to escape the bonds of a social formality that denies what they believe to be their true selves. The quest for intimacy has, at least since the Romantic revolution, been a dominant *cri de coeur*. It has been the source of dramatic revolutionary movements, youth movements, cultural revolutions, and religious innovations and rebellions as well as a plaintive cry of isolated individuals.[9]

The conflict has never diminished, though the organized social and cultural movements that express the demand for reconciliation come and go, as do definitions of the enemies of intimacy. The enemies may be a feudal court, a dynastic aristocracy, petit and haut bourgeoisie, right- and left-wing totalitarianism, bureaucracy, or the isolation of urban life. They may be the church, the office, Victorianism, the court, the neighborhood, the small town, the Party, the market—but always the individual *qua* individual is either repressed or ignored in the full expression of his individuality, or denied the ability to express his "real" self in social situations.

The Intimate and Mass Organization and Culture

The growth of mass education and mass communications, which peculiarly make public the demands for privacy and intimacy, have resulted, over the last 100 to 250 years, in a vast increase in the number of individuals who demand freedom for expression of the private and the intimate. In one sense, the growth of these demands is totally understandable. The growth of large-scale institutions, bureaucracies, and institutions of mass communication and the concentration of organizations in government, in business, and in all spheres of life have weakened the social bonds of institutions of smaller scale, though these latter are not necessarily intimate institutions. A small town, a neighborhood, or a small business is not an institution that in itself provides intimacy. On the contrary, such small-scale institutions, when they are powerful, provide for the dominance of their particular forms of the social, a dominance so strong that, in the extreme, the intimate or private is hard to discover in its environs.

Yet the growth of a wide range of centralized alternative institutions, caused by the decline of the local and the parochial, provides the individual with a sense of alternatives, though not necessarily the means to choose among alternatives. In large-scale institutions one can find countless opportunities for not expressing the private, the intimate, but one is freed from the necessity of accepting any *one* form of public social imperative. Thus, the sense of loss in being "forced" to conform to one set of alternatives because of a variety of possible alternatives is greatest, but such a sense of loss is not the loss of anything one may previously have possessed, except perhaps the loss of the total sense of security and omnipotence one might have had before the age of three. Individuals do not live as historians of their epoch, or in a succession of epochs. They respond to the anguish of the immediate present, and their sense of loss is as great as if that which they lost had ever existed.

The Demand for Intimacy

Regardless of historical causes, the demand for intimacy in social environments that stress public role performance is a real demand, and it is greater now than it has ever been. It is so great because of the expansion of the boundaries and the social and cultural density of those social worlds which are experienced as the cause of the loss of intimacy. These worlds are felt to be distant, external, and, in our sense, nonobligatory. But regardless of the causes of the sense of "alienation," the demand for intimacy persists to the point where it is virtually compulsive. And it exists despite the fact that the social world, whatever its psychological and personal advantages and disadvantages, is the means by which we organize our social production, our existence, and whatever levels of well-being that become the standard from which we experience our discontent. We demand intimacy, and since this demand is obsessional, all too often we fail to see the preconditions and necessities of intimacy. We have indicated that the main necessity is trust. He who would like to be intimate risks exposing himself, his flaws, and his humanity to others who he has reason to believe will like and cherish him to the extent that they will not use the information so divulged as a device to denigrate or exploit him. He assumes that beneath the trust is a level of depth of understanding, love, friendship, or affection that would cause the other to suspend standards of judgment which the other undoubtedly uses in his or her nonintimate social relations. But he who makes such demands for love, affection, and trust can only expect those demands to be at best partially fulfilled. If and when, in the course of a social relationship, one is willing and able to give love, friendship, and trust, the demand implied by such willingness is by itself insufficient to produce its fulfillment. The gift of intimacy requires a noncalculated reciprocal gift. The other must be willing to make the same gifts and make the same demands. And each must be capable of responding not only to his or her own needs and demands but also to the demands of the other. Even if both conditions—the demand and the gift—are present, the achievement of the intimate social relationship is by no means guaranteed, for, tolerance at most is achieved as a result of a conscious social contract. Genuine intimacy occurs only with the passage of time, with repeated social interaction, with the discovery of common intellectual, social, emotional, and cultural responses. And these responses usually emerge slowly, where each social interchange results in increased affection as well as a deepening knowledge of the other.

Trust and Intimacy

The sense of trust is a product of affection and social interchange. As the sense of trust broadens and deepens, each party is able to reveal more of himself, including especially those aspects of the self which in ordinary situations he would conceal because he cannot predict the response, the tolerance, or the love and affection he would receive if he revealed them. To project a sense of the intimate self without this progressive deepening of the social relationship usually invites the risk of a rebuff, because one cannot know in advance of intimacy the level of tolerance and affection or the deeply held standards of the other. But more important, every projection of the intimate self invites a corresponding self-revelation by the other. To blurt out one's intimate self in the absence of the progressive deepening of social relationship is a demand upon the other for reciprocity that the other may be unwilling to meet. And, strangely enough, such self-revelation is, or can be construed as, an invasion of the privacy of the other. The other may respond: "Why should you tell me this, when in exchange I am supposed to make parallel self-revelations? I do not know or like you well enough to tell you my secrets, and therefore I don't want to know yours." Obsessional intimacy, if not prepared for, causes only embarrassment of the other, and therefore a rebuff. At the other extreme is, of course, "feigned intimacy," the projection of pseudo-self-revelation by one party as an invitation to genuine self-relevation by the other. This may be the basis for asymmetric social relations or for the psychological and social dominance of one person by another.

The quest for intimacy in these extreme situations produces a one-sided intimacy, manipulation, and exploitation of the most intimate partner by the other, the less self-revealing one, and after a time an ultimate recognition that one has been "had." If the need for intimacy is obsessional, the individual with such a need may proceed from one asymmetrical relationship to another, always the victim, until untimately he finds either adjustment to victimization in asymmetrical relations or accommodation to a world divided sharply between demands for privacy and an external social objectivity.

Francois Duykaerts offers a similar argument in his study *The Sexual Bond.*[10] He points out, to begin with, that the sexual "instinct" differs from such physiological needs as hunger and elimination in two respects: First, nutrition and elimination needs cannot be long postponed, while humans normally postpone (or are unable to achieve) satisfaction of sexual needs for years at a stretch, and sometimes for a lifetime. One can take a vow of chastity, but similar "vows" with respect to hunger and elimination are not possible. Second, the sexual act is social in a way that the others are not, in that the agreement of another person is necessary. "Before we eat an apple, we do not ask whether it agrees to this fate."

Because of "the special nature of the instinct involved," the question of taking initiative, of responding and negotiating the process of "building a relationship," is psychologically very complicated. The complication arises from what is perhaps the most basic rule of human society, the incest taboo. One lives, in the family, in close proximity with members of the opposite sex who unknowingly provide erotic stimuli; at the same time, the rigid rules governing sexual unions in all human societies mean that for most normal human beings, sexual stimuli will be blocked by powerful psychological controls.

These very deep controls create a state of "normal" inhibition (so that those who lack them may be expected to show deeply pathological or sociopathic forms of behavior). The rules of courtship provided by a given society, then, are not "obstacles" to mating but procedures for the gradual removal of inhibitions through the development of mutual trust and understanding.[11]

In cultures less governed by formal courtship rituals, we may assume that the same negotiation process occurs—the gradual removal of inhibitions between two persons through growing mutual trust and confidence—though varying according to culture and fashion. But however it unfolds, the essential process is one that permits each party to lower his or her defenses and, in the process, to exhibit those weaknesses and infirmities which are normally hidden from all but loving eyes.

Friendship

Sexual intimacy is based upon a combination of physical and psychological intimacy. Our assumption is that the ideal sexual relationship is based on the fusion of the two. Physical intimacy in sex, without psychological intimacy, is most often a perversion of this idea. Usually it requires the falsification of the psychological in order to disguise the physical. To state it differently, when the need for psychological intimacy is great, one can use physical intimacy as a substitute for it. The awareness, more or less conscious, of the greater need of one's partner for psychological intimacy allows the partner with less need to dominate and exploit the other.

Friendship has different bases for intimacy. Close physical intimacy is not a necessity for friendship. To the extent that intimacy is involved in friendship, it is based on personal and psychological affinities. Friendship need not be as deeply intimate as the intimacy that ideally is both physical and psychological.

Friendship can have many bases; it can be based on an attachment to a common value or set of values, or pure sociability; the enjoyment of a set of characteristics that two or more people may share or with which they may complement each other. It may be based on the common fate that a number of individuals may experience together in a hostile environment, or it may be based on a common need to express aspects of the self that are not generally permitted in the public environment. One can say there are positive and negative bases for friendship. The positive aspects are those based on the shared values and experience and the pure enjoyment of the unique aspects of the other's personality and on the enjoyment of the sociability involved in their common activities and personal histories. On the negative side, by means of a common or joint intimate group, individuals can construct group defenses against what is, or is perceived as, a hostile public world.[12]

In the social sciences, and in our previous discussion, we have stressed the term "peer groups" as indicating the sociability and intimacy of equals. Before the rise of the jargon of social science, the word "friendship" might have been used in place of the term "peer groups," but the term "peer group" implies some differences. Peer groups are usually larger social circles than are friendship relationships, though a circle of friends may properly be defined as a "peer group." The term "peer" implies equality; "friendship" does not necessarily have that implication, even though friendship is usually considered to mean the suspension of formal inequalities in the face of common personal attraction. Whether in fact such suspension occurs—and the bases of such suspension is of course always subject to investigation—the problem here is: What are the boundaries to friendship? To what social relationships, milieux, situations, or role demands do intimate friendship demands apply or not apply? When does a friend exceed those boundaries, imposing friendship standards on the formal roles that the friends perform outside their friendship relationships.

Peer Bonds and Official Roles

Two friends, in addition to their informal social relations, may have to deal with each other in nonfriendship roles. They may be officials in the same organization; one may be a seller and the other a buyer or customer. One may be an official, the other a client, or they may be employer and employee. In each such pair of role relations, the demands of friendship may violate the official public roles spelled out by the formal organization and implied in the terms describing the formal relations. The demands of friendship create an expectation for preference upon the friend who, in his formal role, has the power to grant or withhold preference. Role positions usually allow some degree of latitude in the granting of preference, even to a friend. But the boundaries of allowable preference vary in formal organizations and in the amount of allowable "sacrifice" one can make for a friend. Usually the boundaries of preference, while variable, are not clearly demarcated, though at times the official peers and coleagues allow the stretching of official rules for a nonofficial friend.

The demand for preference on the basis of friendship may involve asking the friend to exceed either the official or the informal boundaries incumbent upon him because of his official role. The friend making the demand is not likely to know what the permissible range in behavior allowed his official friend may be. He may be asking the impossible. Or he may be reluctant to ask what is easily grantable because he imagines the boundary of permissible variation in personal demands to be much narrower than the insider knows it to be. Thus a wide range of ambiguities is possible. An official friend may feel insulted when a personal friend does not make demands in cases of need, demands he would readily grant if he knows he can gratify the need. But he may also feel insulted if a friend makes impossible demands; the friend presumes too much on his friendship. The sets of demands, the willingness to communicate both the demand and the need, and the possibility of granting the demand are tests not only of one's official power but of the friendship itself. Unwillingness to communicate a need can be seen as evidence of lack of openness in a friendship; the inability to sense a need can be interpreted as lack of sensitivity in a friendship. The inability to respond to the felt need of the other can be understood as a lack of strength of the friendship. Finally, unwillingness to accept the inability of a friend to respond to a need can be interpreted as either lack of trust in the friendship or lack of knowledge upon which such trust can be based. Yet all these ambiguities are based ultimately on the sensitivity of each member in a friendship pair or group to the needs of the other, and an ability to communicate the needs and the response to the needs of the other in such ways that each party can know and trust the response of the other.

Peer Groups and Intimacy

Peer groups are likely to have an informal structure that approaches formal recognition. Like friendship role relationships, the peer group may be a gang, a clique, a bloc, or a network often having manifest functions that are objective in character. These functions include the monopolization of turf, the division of spoils, or mutual support in career aspirations and in defense against formal authority or public institutions. All peer groups are based on a recognition of the individual *qua* individual. Their members demand and give loyalty and personal support for each other as individuals. In their own way, however, they may create a quasi-public set of standards for the members of the group, which may be more pervasive, more totalitarian, and more demanding than those of public institutions. We have indicated that the "failure" of public institutions may be that they demand less of the individual than does the peer group. That is, they express less of the total personality of the individuals who are its members than those individuals would want to have expressed. Thus the individual seeks both more intimate friendships than are allowed in public life and the expression of those aspects of his self that are not publicly recognized. In all of these ways, the peer group resembles and is based upon networks of personal friendships.

Networks

A network can be defined as a social linkage of friends or peers in which not all of the friends know each other. Each member of the network may be able to make informal or network "role" demands on another by virtue of his connection (friendship or intimacy) to one or more third parties in the network. Not all friendships or peer relationships within a network are equally strong, nor are the demands that can be made upon others in a network. Moreover, a network is unlikely to have clear-cut boundaries. It consists only of "friends of friends," so that no one person is likely to know all the friends of one's friends, and, in turn, their friends and *their* friends' friends. The network is operative only to the extent that one makes demands upon it, and to the extent that these demands are recognized, accepted, and honored. It becomes inoperative at the points where no demands are made or they are rejected. For example, the demands of friendship may be "stretched too far." At that point a distant network member may say: "Why should I give preference to a friend of a friend of a friend whom I don't know or care about?"

Networks are not "groups" that have clear-cut boundaries and relatively clear-cut reciprocal role relations; they are, as Yablonsky has called them, "near groups."[13]

Peer Groups and Friendship

The term *network* describes the operation and circulation of friendship relationships in a more or less "diluted" form. Peer group relations operate somewhat differently, in that there is a vast variety for the basis of peer groups. During the period of adolescence, peer groups may be the most open and the most subject to personal intimacy. Adolescents use peer groups to express emergent gropings for personal autonomy and growth, and dissatisfaction with the constraints that both childhood and adulthood press upon them. At earlier periods peer groups may primarily express resentments of the constraints imposed upon their members by authority, by parents and other adults.[14] At later stages peer groups may be semi-organized groups to accommodate the joint aspirations of their members and appear to be exchanges of personal support and recognition in the respective members' desires to enter an establishment or to achieve success. At still other times, and at all ages, especially the adult years, peer groups represent a joint effort on the part of individuals to recapture a sense of intimacy, sociability, and relaxation from the constraints of either the formal requirements or the hostile environment of the public worlds one is forced to live in. Again, friendship has many of these characteristics. Yet there are differences. First of all, the requirements of friendship tend to be far less structured than those of peer groups. Friendship can operate on almost any level, and even across levels.

Friendship and the Bounds of Intimacy

Persons may be friends in the pursuit of a single value or interest —in a love for music, perhaps, or bowling, or the telling of jokes. While such friendships are not necessarily based upon the requirements of public roles, they do not demand deep levels of intimacy. In fact, once an understanding of the basis of the friendship emerges, one of the requirements of the friendship is that the parties not intrude beyond the understood boundaries of their particular friendship. Such friendships may not require a great deal of emphasis on privacy, in the sense that a deep revelation of self is not required, nor is one necessarily intimate with the other in terms of one's total self. The quality of privacy here is *privacy from the public world* rather than *privacy for the personal world*. Yet in the sense that one has common values and a common sense of attraction, the quality of friendship is important in that it allows an opportunity for the expression of aspects of the self that are often denied in the public world.

This does not mean that all friendships are of this order; rather, the characteristic of friendship is that it can be established on almost any basis of intimacy, ranging perhaps from the friendship of convenience to total psychological intimacy.

The friendship of convenience can be illustrated by the office friendship: a group or pair of individuals who choose, during the course of the day or during lunch or coffee breaks, to gossip, shop, or hang out together. Such friendships may not be operative after work hours or on weekends and, moreover, are not expected to be. The "demands" of such friendships are related only to work or to the working day. At the other extreme are the friendships that allow for the total expression of the intimate self in the form of self-revelation; again, with the expectation of tolerance, affection, and the suspension of normal standards of judgment.

The Boundaries of Friendship

Given this wide range in form and content of friendship, it is difficult to formulate the "rules" for describing friendship. Then "rules" may mean a minimal inquiry into the deeply private and intimate life of the other or the tact to avoid questioning the behavior and life of the other. They may also include the avoidance of burdening a limited contract of friendship by projecting more of oneself into the relationship than the implied boundaries suggest.

The nature of these boundaries, however, is not given in advance. That is to say, any friendship can begin on a limited basis and can progress to one of total psychological intimacy. The boundaries may be discovered by the avoidance of some topics and by some degrees of self-revelation by one party, so that he can see from the avoidance by the other what level of self-revelation or selection of the basis of a friendship is appropriate. The boundaries may be defined by the failure of one party to respond to the self-revelation of the other, which chokes off further discussion. In extreme situations the boundaries are established by explicit interdiction of discussion or by quarrels: "You have no right to tell me that" or, "Please don't tell me that, I don't want to know." These forms of limitation of friendship may establish the scale of breadth and depth of any friendship. Depending on where the lines are drawn, the quality of a particular friendship is established. At the same time, we can repeat that there are no *necessary* limits on the boundaries of friendship, though by definition we are excluding sexual liaisons as being, *per se*, an expression of the pure form of friendship. If sexual intimacy is involved, then we by definition treat it as a different category. This of course does not mean that there may be, at deeper levels, no sexual attraction in friendship, nor that manifest sexual liaisons may not preclude aspects of friendship.*

Friendship and "Mobility"

Of course, the limited forms of friendship based on comfort, self-assurance, and the necessity of projecting images of past achievement are possible only for those whe have reached levels of achievement sufficient to project an image of success. Not all individuals have the necessary success to provide such projections. This is true despite the fact that age in itself often provides minimal standards of achievement which allow such elements of self-satisfaction to emerge. Moreover, individuals are likely to select such social environments and patterns of friendship and social interchange that allow them to feel comfortable in their personal milieu. Given the fact that each individual has a personal history, has emerged from adolescence in peer groups where some degree of mobility is expected of him—at least in middle-class society—differential social achievement inevitably takes place. Given the pyramidal structure of societies, some individuals—whatever the standards used—are not equally successful.[15] Moreover, lack of success can be personified in their relative failure as compared with siblings, with classmates, with adolescent peers. Since relative success is often a standard by which individuals judge each other, especially individuals known to each other from a common starting point, the fact of relative failure often constitutes a source of humiliation.[16] The amount of possible humiliation is judged on the basis of the "promise," i.e., the prediction, that one's

---

*Friendships that have a latent sexual component (whether heterosexual or homosexual) represent a psychologically complicated boundary case. If and when the sexual component is acted out, in our terms it ceases to be a case of friendship. If it is not acted out but is present in the nonsexual social relation of the friends, then a new dimension is added to the friendship. Thus, the friendship may include elements of courtship, jealousy, and quasi-sexual play on the one hand, and avoidance, taboo, and excessive delicacy and tact on the other hand. Both kinds of sexual element, of course, radically alter the nature of a friendship.

friends, teachers, and family made for a youth who subsequently fell short of their predictions. In his maturity, the middle years, when the relatively successful celebrate their achievements in the relaxed sociability that occurs after achievement has been reached, and when the lessened desire or possibility for further achievement diminishes the work demands that individuals place upon themselves—in these situations, those who are not modestly successful experience humiliation in social terms for not being successful. Quite frequently they cannot participate in the social activities of their former peers, because the costs of such participation—membership fees, admissions, recreational costs—are far too great. Moreover, the relatively unsuccessful are likely not to acquire the self-confidence, the poise, and the polish that both accompany are evidence of success. They are not able to exhibit any social contacts with more successful persons in conversation and gossip about successful persons with whom they associate. Such name-dropping often embellishes a successful career. The unsuccessful are less likely to make references to vacations, travel, fine restaurants and hotels, and other indicators of success. They are likely to experience all such references as boasting, as insult, as competitive gestures which they are not able to answer. Finally, they are likely to see themselves as objects of pity, sympathy, and condescension; they are likely to feel excluded from really important activities and included only as a means of enhancing the success of the other. They may be right.

All of the above does not deny the power of adolescent friendship. The friendship ties of adolescence may cut across differences in mobility, in success, and in subsequent life experience, so that they may remain the primary basis for the mutual identity of a friendship pair. The successful person may devalue his success because he may at some levels concede that his success was due to his possession of relatively unimportant qualities: the ability to lie, to smile, to exploit opportunities regardless of the ethics involved, to focus his self into those channels which are the gateway to opportunity, and to discipline himself to those aspects of maturity which deny the youthful talents that he shared in adolescence with his less successful friend. He may feel that he has been successful in selling out and that his friend lacked this talent. Moreover, the road chosen by his less successful friend may have been far more rocky and difficult, and the lack of success may be a tribute to the other's integrity and persistence in a valued but unrewarded activity. He may recognize all the virtues in his friend that were present in that friend's youthful promise and are neither corrupted nor recognized by others in the present. The unsuccessful friend may be able to recognize the successful one as having "deep down, underneath," the same talents that he had as a youth. And both may treasure their reciprocal talents. For the unsuccessful friend, the capacity to value the other must be based on his ability to suspend his bitterness at his own lack of success and to avoid projecting too strongly the notion that the other's success is based on either luck or betrayal of talent. The successful friend must be able to avoid projecting the notion that he values the other's continued friendship as a means of celebrating his own success. At the same time, he must avoid condescension and exclusion, which would embarrass or insult his friend; but he also must avoid the kind of inclusion that might be interpreted as constituting a source of embarrassment to his friend. Thus, friendship across the barriers of relative success and failure require sensitivity, tact, and awareness, as well as genuine love and affection. The possible sources of estrangement are, needless to say, great. In all probability the vast majority of adolescent friendships become attentuated over time. Peer group relationships tend to reorganize and reassemble themselves in terms of the current basis of equality implicit in the term *peer.* This is not surprising. What is perhaps surprising is the fact that many adolescent peer relations persist beyond these conditions of physical and social distance. It seems to us that the persistence of such friendships is one of the highest achievements of our species.

But beyond such accomplishments, the persistence of peer friendship provides—one hopes unintentionally—a basis for a stable set of identities that enables the individual to say that he has a self. In other words, we could all become totally different persons as a result of the differential experience of success, and each major achievement or failure could constitute the basis for the reconstituting one's total personality on the basis of success of failure. This would include the selection of new friends, new intimates, new values, preferences, and activities, all on the basis of the purposive activities leading to success and to the vagaries of success. If this were always the case, we would become totally different persons at each stage in our social and economic careers, and nothing would tie the personality together, except the inability to repress inconvenient memories* and the ulcers and psychological problems that occur

*The same analysis would apply to changes in marital partners and, to some extent, to one's children, following divorce and remarriage in which the new partner and children are appropriate to the stages in one's career.

when such repression takes place. Our ulcers and psychological problems may be a better indicator of the persistence of identity than the cognitive rational social relations that are appropriate to ever reconstituted and new identities.

Quite obviously, many of us do reconstitute our personalities on the basis of the poise, self-confidence, and self-assurance—or lack thereof—accompanying success or failure, and many of us reconstitute our identities on the ever changing set of information, skills, and emerging and developing talents that accompanies one's movement through the milieux that are the results of success or lack thereof. But the persistence of friendship, of old established relationships based on the common history and experience of two friends, signifies the continuity of the self and the unwillingness of the individuals in question to surrender their historical selves in exchange for the current demands of an ever moving present.

A final kind of friendship as related to the experience of differential success is the friendship based on failure. Individuals who may not have been close in the past but in the present find themselves (or believe they find themselves) in the common situation of being excluded, condescended to, humiliated, or otherwise treated as failures, may form friendships based on resentment. Their social bond may consist in the conversational exposure of the sneers and condescension of their friends, of the fraudulent activity that is or was the basis of their success, of the hyprocrisy in the parading of the symbols of success and the lack of genuineness revealed in their current activities ("I knew him when he . . ."). The opportunity to express such evidence of resentment can be made only to a spouse who is forced to share the lack of success of her mate or to another unsuccessful friend, whether of old or recent standing, whose equivalent lack of success will make one's own complaints and resentments an appropriate topic of conversation. For the successful person who is not unusually tolerant the complaints engendered of resentment are likely to be considered at best "sour grapes" and at worst a personal insult. Yet even the sharing of relative failure in intimate groups constitutes a defense of the self against a hostile world, where lack of success is regarded as proof of lack of manhood, a source of guilt and self-abasement.

Notes

1. See Hans Gerth and C. Wright Mills, *From Max Weber* (New York: Oxford University Press, (1946): "The Social Psychology of the World Religions," "The

Protestant Sects and the Spirit of Capitalism," and "Religious Rejections of the World and their Directions." Also Max Weber, *The Sociology of Religion,* trans. Ephraim Fischoff (Boston: Beacon Press, 1963), and *idem, Economy and Society,* ed. Guenther Roth and Claus Wittich (New York: Bedminster Press 1968), vol. 2, chapter VI.

2. See Joseph Bensman and Arthur Vidich, *The New American Society—The Revolution of the Middle Class* (Chicago: Quadrangle Books, 1971), on inter-institutional power cliques and other informal "friendship" groups, pp. 88-98.

3. Goffman, *Asylums,* especially "On the Characteristics of Total Institutions." See also Max Weber's essay, "The Social Causes of the Decay of Ancient Civilization," to be found in several sources: trans. Christian Mackauer, in *Journal of General Education* V (1950): 75-88; also in part IV of Weber, *The Agrarian Sociology of Ancient Civilizations,* as "The Social Causes of the Decline of Ancient Civilizations," trans. R. I. Frank (London: NLB, 1976). The Mackauer translation is also reprinted in J. E. T. Eldridge, ed., *Max Weber: The Interpretation of Social Reality* (New York: Scribner's, 1971).

4. Joseph Bensman and Bernard Rosenberg, *Mass, Class, and Bureaucracy* (Englewood Cliffs, N.J.: Prentice-Hall, 1963), Chapter Six, "The Urban Community," esp. p. 160, "Antiurban Social Theory"; in the second version of this work (New York: Praeger, 1976), see Chapter 5, "The Community," pp. 135-137, "Historical Antiurbanism."

5. "When someone has behaved like an animal, he says: 'I'm only human!' But when he is treated like an animal, he says: 'I'm human, too!'" Karl Kraus, *Half-Truths and One-and-a-Half-Truths: Selected Aphorisms,* ed. and trans. Harry Zohn (Montreal: Engendra Press, 1976), p. 108. For further details, see Victor Lasky: *It Didn't Start with Watergate* (New York: Dial Press, 1977); *idem, JFK: The Man and the Myth* (New York: Macmillan, 1963); and *idem, RFK: The Myth and the Man* (New York: Trident, 1968).

6. Lasky, *It Didn't Start with Watergate,* pp. 81-85, *et passim.*

7. Sigmund Freud, *Civilization and Its Discontents,* trans. James Strachey (New York: Norton, 1961), pp. 52-54.

8. Francois Duyckaerts, *The Sexual Bond,* trans. John A. Kay (New York: Dell Books, 1970), pp. 24-32 and 205-215. See also pp. 155-158 below.

9. Marshall Berman, *The Politics of Authenticity,* and Lionel Trilling, *Sincerity and Authenticity.* Also Emmanuel Mounier, *Personalism,* trans. Philip Mairet (London: RKP, 1952; reprint, Notre Dame, Ind.: University of Notre Dame Press, n.d.): ". . . we are expected to sigh over the lost little communities—the village, the workshop and the family—and to disseminate fear of the greater associations. There are grave misunderstandings in this attitude. It implies an abuse of the mystique of *nearness* as well as of *smallness.* Whenever man has had to confront an enlargement of his sphere of action, he has been seized by the same panic, the same feeling of being menaced or rendered derelict." ". . . this anti-collectivism conceals an underlying nostalgia for a puristic notion of a society of persons which is impossible. In practical fact, a communication is generally delegated" (pp. 25-26).

10. Duyckaerts, *Sexual Bond*, pp. 6–20.

11. *Ibid.*, Chapters I, VI, and VII.

12. For a similar discussion, see C. S. Lewis, "Friendship" (chapter IV), in *The Four Loves* (New York: Harcourt Brace Jovanovich, 1960): "It is therefore easy to see why Authority frowns on Friendship. Every real Friendship is a sort of secession, even a rebellion. It may be a rebellion of serious thinkers against accepted claptrap or of faddists against accepted good sense; of real artists against popular ugliness or of charlatans against civilised taste; of good men against the badness of society or of bad men against its goodness. Whichever it is, it will be unwelcome to Top People. In each knot of Friends there is a section 'public opinion' which fortifies its members against the public opinion of the community in general. Each therefore is a pocket of potential resistance. Men who have real Friends are less easy to manage or 'get at'; harder for good Authorities to correct or for bad Authorities to corrupt. Hence if our masters, by force or by propaganda about 'togetherness' or by unobtrusively making privacy and unplanned leisure impossible, ever succeed in producing a world in which all are Companions and none are Friends, they will have removed certain dangers, and will also have taken from us what is almost our strongest safeguard against complete servitude" (pp. 114–15).

13. See note 2 above; see also Lewis Yablonsky, "The Violent Gang or a Near Group" (chapter 14) in *The Violent Gang,* rev. ed. (New York: Macmillan, 1962).

14. Jean Piaget, *The Language and Thought of the Child,* trans. Marjorie Gabain (New York: Meridian Books, 1975; reprint, 1966), Chapters 2 and 3.

15. Melvin Tumin and Arnold Feldman, "Theory and Measurement of Occupational Mobility," *American Sociological Review,* XXII, no. 3, (1957): 281–88.

16. Richard Sennett and Jonathan Cobb, *The Hidden Injuries of Class* (New York: Random House, 1972; Vintage Books reprint, 1973), especially Part II: "Dreams and Defenses."

Chapter 5

Privacy, Intimacy, and the Life Cycle

In previous chapters we have dwelt upon the emergence of social roles that are traditional—public, private, and intimate. We have attempted to do so in terms of the evolving history of social institutions and of culture. But the problem of privacy can also be understood in terms of the life cycle of the individual, at least minimally separated from these larger social frameworks.

Privacy can be understood initially in terms of the biological nature of the organism. The experience of pain is a private phenomenon; no person can directly experience another's physical pain. One can, however, empathize with the pain of another and can experience a secondary sympathetic pain. The observer, seeing an expression of pain in an individual, can, from the recollection of his own pain, imagine the pain of another. But it is his own past pain that he is imagining, not the physical experience of the other's pain. Sympathetic pain is qualitatively different from primary physiological pain.

In the same way there are some forms of pleasure, of euphoria, that are intensely private. One can, through the projection of pleasure, produce a sympathetic pleasure in the other that is social, but that social pleasure is a new element in the situation. That is, we frequently are able to share in the joy of others even when we do not know exactly what the other's joy is about, and often it is far more convenient to us to be joyful, to share in the joy of others, than to inquire into the source of the joy, especially when such extreme joyfulness presents itself without explanation. So, when one asks the observer what he is happy about in such a situation, all he can say is that he is happy because everybody else is happy. Only the original communicator of the joy may know what its cause is, and only he can experience its uniqueness. The others respond to his expression, his inner glow, animation, the feeling he communicates. The initial expression gives off an aura of emotionality that communicates itself to others. The others must respond to that aura, not to the joy-giving experience itself, and they respond in terms of the manifestations of the experience and emotion rather than to the experience.

In extreme cases the original communicator of joy or pain may not know the source of his emotion. The joy or pain is so private that it is kept secret from its bearer. In Freudian terms, the id as a source of energy or the pleasure principle and thanatos (the death instinct) are unconscious, operate at the deepest level of inwardness, and are not available to the conscious self. The deepest sense of privacy is the unconscious. The individual cannot communicate it directly because he does not know it. Others may sense the results of one's unconscious. They may know that something is "wrong" or that an individual may not know what he is doing or saying. They may guess at the unconscious meanings, but they cannot be sure if their guesses are right. Most important, they cannot respond directly and consciously to the person in terms of that person's unconscious motives and actions.

But whether one is a Freudian or not, almost all expressive terms and all symbolic expression develop levels of incommunicability that cannot be expressed in significant signs. The resonances of these terms evoke emotional responses, which are felt at such levels of subjectivity that they must be considered to be felt in private. At the same time, the sympathetic evocation of similar symbols, words, or gestures, or of the same ones among a number of people, suggests that such language produces common sympathetic but private responses. The purely private is transformed in producing symbols and images that stimulate a parallel private response. Occasionally, however, the quality of the intended private response is revealed when one learns its basis and intellectually knows that the appropriate emotional response ought to be forthcoming, but in fact feels nothing. The terms conventionally used to evoke deep subjective private feelings fail to produce those feelings. At the other extreme, one can pretend to give off the signs of deep private concern by simulating their social manifestation in facial or body gestures. At this point, the private becomes so socialized, so objectified, that it can exist in social, objective terms, without existing as a private phenomenon: The social expression is a screen to a void. Mime as a dramatic form or as dance, in Kabuki or Balinese dancing, objectifies the facial and bodily expression of pleasure and pain, as does much religious ritual. These deep expressions of subjectivity are so imbedded in extremely objective, formal gestures that no "personal" communication is necessary. But the ability to counterfeit the manifestations of privacy is evidence that this absolute privacy may exist.

At the other extreme, we are often called upon to repress sympathetic responses to the pain of others in order to assure the other that the pain they feel is not noticed. When someone commits a social *gaffe,* a really horrible blunder, kindness requires us not to act as if we are sympathetically embarrassed, because in doing so we remind the other of his *gaffe.* Or, when we encounter the manifestation of pain in others, in situations where we feel that the expression of pain is part of a disease, a disorder, or a delusion, we may choose to suppress any sympathetic response in order not to encourage the person to continue in a direction that we feel is unwise, foolish, or dangerous. If a person is acting in a paranoid way, we may choose not to sympathize or support what we regard as his delusions, in the belief that our support will only strengthen the delusions. We do this even though we know that the paranoid delusion is symptomatic of intense pain. In the other direction, we may go so far as to support the delusion in extreme ways, to exaggerate it and by so doing to make it appear to be absurd in order to underline the delusional character of the projected fantasy. We may paradigmatically say, "Yes, the underworld, including people who have never seen or known you, are out to steal your few paltry bucks, and they are investing millions of dollars in the attempt to steal your hundreds." We act unsympathetically, using mock sympathy as a device to communicate a far deeper and more genuine sympathy. Yet, in doing so, we recognize the private nature of the pain, though we are not able at the moment to discover its sources or to respond to the primary nature of the pain.

Sympathetic experiencing of the private feelings of others can be carried to such extremes that in doing so the individual represses knowledge and sensation of his own private experience. He lives vicariously through the defeats and victories of others, attempting to imagine their pleasure and pain. Yet the ultimate incommunicability of such primary experience is so absolute that the individual so afflicted neither experiences the private sensations of others nor has access to his own private feelings. He may use a pseudo-sympathy for another as a devise to avoid his own feelings. We recognize the emptiness of such behavior by the embarrassment we sometimes feel for the lack of ability of the individual to experience his own life. Since he is so obtuse in his borrowing of others' feelings, and communicates only such borrowings, the others reject him and make him the butt of jokes and sneers. Such men without qualities are a standard butt in literature for sadism, more so than they are in daily life.[1] In daily life they are usually merely a source of embarrassment.

The Objectification of the Biologically Private

The infant, from the moment of birth, and progressively through myelation, has the capacity to experience biological pain and the forms of euphoria associated with physical gratification and well-being (primary narcissism), but he lacks the capacity to provide conscious expression of the form and content and source of his emotions. His expression is at most involuntary. The parent or the surrogate parent must, on the basis of his/her sympathetic response, project into the infant the feelings and background for them he/she imagines the infant is involuntarily expression. He/she can only partially project himself/herself into the emotional life of the infant other. To the extent that he/she succeeds by his/her actions in alleviating the pain or in reinforcing the pleasure, he/she succeeds in communicating. But more than this, he/she ultimately channels, primarily by adding to the infant's nonverbal gestures the vocabulary that expresses in part the infant's emotion. In part the adult defines the source of pain or pleasure, and in part he or she provides the terminology and the action that expresses or corrects the situation. The adult provides the objectivity and social expression of what originates in the purely private physiological and biological spheres.[2] If all of these processes went smoothly and if the need and the intended results were in phase, there would be few problems. Unfortunately, the capacity of the infant to absorb such instruction is limited, as is the empathetic as well as the manifest capacity of the adult to understand the primitive gestures of the child. The adult is impaired in these efforts by his/her own obstacles to understanding, which are often the result of his/her own impaired socialization.[3] Moreover, the child's demands, based in deep psychological and physiological motiviations, may be ultimately impossible to gratify. If the child in effect points and says: "Daddy, give me the moon," the father may find gratification difficult, or he man be reluctant to explain to a one-year-old that, despite the child's illusions, he is not strong or tall enough to give him the moon. Nor is he willing to risk making the explanation for his inadequacy. The child is bound to express needs that are incapable of gratification, and the parent is incapable of communicating his inability to gratify these needs. The failure of communication means that some private meanings and deeply felt emotions are not capable of expression, even by the child to himself, for the terms in which self-communication are ultimately rendered are themselves the product of communication and clarification by adults. The child thus does not learn the whole meaning of the urges and tensions that govern much of his action, and his failure to learn may produce secondary resentments, angers, and blockages which he may not be able to express. That is, he may not want to express, even to himself, the resentments and frustrations that are provoked by an all-powerful parent, who in many other areas is to be loved and cherished. These secondary emotions of aggression, resentment, and hostility become repressed and are often inaccessible to the infant, and therefore part of that kind of privacy that in most cases is incapable of being expressed even to the self. They also constitute a cause for further blockages in communication.

In any event, the weakness and dependency of the human infant is such that every function of the infant, biological and social, must be governed by the intervention of an adult. Elimination and urination, of course, are beyond the control of the individual; but one's biological and social incompetency are also subject to continuous observation, interference, and intervention. To the individual in the first months of existence, such lack of privacy is of no great concern, for the growth of the private individual to the stage where he can resent the lack of privacy has not yet occurred. The parent or supervising adult, while intervening in these biological functions of the individual, attempts to develop the infant's competence, so that further intervention may ultimately become unnecessary. But there is no way that the withdrawal of intervention into the private life of the individual can develop exactly in phase with the growth of personal competence. Hence the developing child begins to resent the intrusion into his privacy exactly as he develops a private self. And this is especially true when the individual is expected to develop a private self as a concomitant of maturation and personal competence. The child then must in effect say, "Let me do it by myself. Stop interfering and let me do it by myself, even in your absence."

And when he does do it—in the absence of others—he becomes a private individual. From the standpoint of the other, the achievement of personal competence and of privacy in the child means that the other must surrender the right to intervene, to observe, to direct, and therefore must surrender some of his authority over the growing child, where in the initial stage his authority seemed to be complete.

Unwillingness to surrender such authority means the continuous invasion of privacy by the adult, all occurring at levels far beyond the simple physiological level and development of motor competence so far described. For the development of the self, i.e., the private self, rests on the individual's taking over completely the attitude of the other, developing his own standards, in Freudian terms a super-ego.[4] The raw materials for such internalization is not complete until the individual no longer needs the physical presence of others to provide the standards of others, or to continuously reinforce them. But complete internalization means the use of internalized standards, even against those persons who are the source of the standards. If the parent succeeds in implanting the ideal of absolute honesty in his children, he should not be surprised when the children use these standards against him. The parent may find it difficult or confusing to the child when he or she tries to teach the child not to lie when lying may be protective of other interests of the child. More poignantly, the parent, having taught honesty to the child, subjects himself to the child's sense of outrage, when he allows the child to witness situations where the parent is obviously lying, even lying to the child. Or, even more important, the parent reaches the stage in "socializing" the child where his success at previous self-projections makes further self-projection unnecessary or intolerable. The child has learned enough and now needs to "practice" by himself. At this level, the development of privacy in the child results in a desire on the child's part for a restriction on the right of a parent to invade the child's privacy. The surrender of power involved in successful socialization may be intuitively recognized by the parent as too great a loss of previously recognized power. The parent may need the sense of direct power to reassure himself of his sense of omnipotence in his parental role. In such cases, the parent may socialize the child to dependency. This may be accomplished by continuous cross-examination of the child, by providing continuously contradictory directives which require endless clarification, by inviting, soliciting, or demanding continuous self-revelation on the part of the child under the threat of withdrawal of love, or by continuously analyzing the behavior of the child in the child's presence. In doing the latter, the parents make the child a public self-analyst, using "socialization" as an excuse. The child learns to treat his most private feelings as public property.[5]

At another level, the parent may encourage self-revelation, the surrender of privacy by the child, through his own self-revelation and surrender of privacy to the child. He or she encourages the child to "confess" by providing his/her own prior confession to the child. Thus, the parent becomes a child in order to keep the child in childhood, In such situations, both child and parent create no boundaries for the self, no boundaries within which privacy exists. But this is an impossible task, because biologically the individual is a private person, in the sense, as we have previously defined it, of experiencing pleasure, pain, expressive language, competence or incompetence, as private phenomena.

The lack of privacy created by these attempts at personality absorption does not result in the destruction of privacy; rather it results in the "overaccessibility" of the individual's private feeling to one's self. The individual attempts to analyze each feeling, emotion, and thought and to render it in intellectual terms. The intellectualization of the deeply subjective, the personal, and the emotional results in the destruction of the capacity to feel those emotions whose substitutes are pale intellectualized renditions. Words replace feelings, and feelings are made empty of their original content. We are uneasy or horrified when a child speaks in too adult a fashion of feelings which most properly ought not be exposed or, if expressed, ought to be spoken in language less "wordy," articulate, or rational.[6] To some degree it used to be considered improper to reveal too much of one's deeper feelings in highly intellectual abstract terms before an audience so distant from the person that the expression of such feelings could not matter to the audience. Thus, wearing one's heart on one's sleeve was considered bad taste, but not quite so bad as wearing a synthetic heart on one's sleeve.

Sibling Relationships and Privacy

The initial desires to achieve a self, whether successful or not, are aimed at separating the self from that of the parent or parental substitute. These desires may originate in the attempt of the child to achieve that independence and autonomy, that sense of power, that the child observes and admires in the parent. They may be based in part on imitation and identification. But, regardless of these motives, they result in conflict. As we have noted, one set of conflicts results from the unwillingness of the parent to let go, expressed through the invasion of privacy. At times, the attempts at achieving a private self despite the invasions of privacy by the parental invaders can be accomplished by surrendering one's privacy to another set of persons. The willing surrender of privacy we have called intimacy. The individual voluntarily makes the offer of his self, his private world, in the form of intimacy with others, for furtherance of the attempts to resist the invasion of privacy by unwelcome invaders. He establishes intimate relations as a support for an emerging sense of privacy. The psychological point is that this will permit the expression—to one's self as well as to the intimate other—of materials and wishes that, if expressed to the invading parent, would call forth censure, control, and punishment.

In its simplest terms, the surrender of privacy is most frequently made among siblings. In such cases the siblings align themselves with each other, deny the parents access to their selves, and organize vast and complex camouflages, which result in a social conspiracy to prevent deeper observation, detailed supervision, and constant regulation by parents. To some degree this may occur among brothers and sisters who are relatively close in age, but once established it will persist through the lifetime of the siblings. There are, however, some dangers to these intimate relations. The parties to the conspiracy have already been necessarily subject to the invasion of their privacy that is implicit in all socialization by adults. Not only is each child subject to the scrutiny of his behavior by the parents, but he frequently is called upon, or may want, to report the behavior of his siblings to their parents. Such reported observation may be the basis for discipline and regulation by the parent. Each brother or sister acts in this way as a surrogate parent. In revealing one's self to the sibling one may risk either direct or indirect exposure of one's self to the parent. At times this is often desired; the child who does not wish to confront the parent directly may reveal himself to the "sneaky" brother and sister who will communicate to the parent what the original communicator will not do directly. At times, his self-revelation through a third party may not be part of a conscious plan; yet, had the individual thought of it, he would have known that his self-revelation was inevitable. Beyond this, each sibling is usually a rival for a parent's favor, and each child learns, as do his brothers and sisters, that their brothers and sisters are, at times, "squealers." The process of revelation to a sibling becomes, after some experience, a highly controlled display of his intimate self. The individual retains a private sense of self despite selective self-revelation and selective intimacy with a sibling.

Privacy and the Peer Group

The conspiracy between siblings to shut out the parents involves the maximization of intimacy by siblings but can be fully achieved only when all children are united in equal hostility or resistance to the parents. Such situations, however, are rare. In their absence, siblings prove to be relatively unsatisfactory intimates. Peers are far more satisfactory as counterweights to an enforced intimacy with parents or as a means of developing privacy at the expense of one's family. But again, the achievement of this kind of privacy is accomplished by the surrender of the sense of the private self to age- and sex-graded intimates. Peers are superior to siblings in that each peer is an agent a distant and unrelated elder. They are not rivals for the same affections, nor do they have equal access to the same parents. Moreover, membership in peer groups is optional; it is possible to exclude the "squealer" and to make demands among a group of peers for collective privacy, that is, it involves an intimacy that precludes elders and other family members. It emerges where such exclusiveness is not possible among siblings, especially when the peer group member is too young to leave the home.

Beyond this, the use of intimacy allows the individual to present to his peer mates' information, experience, and observations, which are not reportable to parents because parental standards are such that they regard possession of such information with distaste or as a punishable offense. It is for this reason that peer groups among children through the phase of young adulthood always have a semi-illicit flavor. They exist in resistance to the parents and to the constituted agents of authority. Other factors contribute to the quasi-illegality, to the anti-establishment aura of peer-group intimacy. When parents are of a different social class from their children—i.e., when the parents have been mobile, and the children are born or raised after the achievement of parental mobility—the parents represent a different world of cultural as well as of age-bound experiences; the children, who live in a one-class world, can respond to each other in terms of styles of thought which the parents, perhaps because of their more varied background, cannot share. This is obviously more clearly the case when the parents have different national backgrounds (are migrants or immigrants) from their children's. The parents may represent standards that are devalued in the entire nonfamily world of the children. The difference in standards, experience, culture, and patterns of thought may be so great that children cannot (or will not) communicate with parents, and vice versa. The nonfamily world in Western urban society may constitute much more of the context of daily life for the children than does their family world. Peer groups thus provide a locus of intimacy for their members that the family cannot provide. They provide privacy at the expense of the parents. Because of similar separation of worlds, the same uses can be made of peer groups with respect to all other adults: teachers, preachers, youth leaders, policemen, and even age-mates who respond favorably to adult standards. The anti-establishment aura of the peer group becomes generalized.

To repeat ourselves, the privacy that individuals attain in the process of socialization is balanced by the development of peer intimacy and a surrender of the self to one's peers. A privacy that is dependent on peer groups is not genuine, since it is a collective and not an individual privacy. In fact, the peer group frequently requires that the individual reveal all and subject himself to the collective demands of a group for the surrender of the total self to the group.[7]

If the individual becomes habituated to this form of intimacy, he may become incapable of ever achieving genuine privacy in the sense that an individual responds primarily to himself in the process of responding to others. David Riesman would call this being "other-oriented." Yet the development of peer-group membership is frequently a necessary stage in the development of a sense of self. But if the development of the individual is arrested at this stage, then he never quite becomes an individual. He remains dependent on finding and becoming a member of a group to which he wants to or cannot help but surrender himself; if the need is too great, it matters little what his standards are. More than that, the peer group has definite standards to which one can surrender.

Adolescent Peer Groups

Yet one cannot dismiss peer groups so easily, for peer groups exist at all age levels, and membership in peer groups over time is related to the experience of typical problems in the life cycle of the individual. The experience of puberty involves dealing with one's own emerging sexuality, one's own attempt to deal as a sexual person with sexually attractive persons of the same or opposite sex. The ability to report success or failure and to learn successful social and sexual technique from someone who is willing to support and teach and who will support one in one's failures and respond to one's successes, at both the social and the sexual level, becomes a necessity, especially as parents and most elders are not willing, able, or desirable as audiences for such "confessions." Therefore, as Erikson properly points out, the only groups so available are peer groups.[8]

Of course, the mastery of one's own sexuality and the response to failure and success in attempts to deal with it are only one possible basis for the emergence of peer groups. Every new stage in one's adolescent career provides new levels of anxiety, new levels of estrangement. The estrangement is from a world one has outgrown as well as from one that is not yet achieved, and from a world that represents one's deeply internalized infantile past. At any point in this set of moving incongruities, the worlds of past and future represent and contain negative possibilities, but the world of the present is fraught with anxieties. The world of the present represents a test of previously untested talents, the achievement of new levels of personal competence, the acquisition of social and technical skills, the mastery of performance skills, and the ability to present onself in desired terms to others regardless of one's insecurities and anxieties.

To the undeveloped person, overcoming these ambiguities and anxieties requires social support. Parents are often unavailable because their hopes for their children constitute an added obstacle, added freight which the child must bear. Pep talks by a successful adult quite frequently seem irrelevant to an anxiety-ridden youngster, for the successful adult appears unable to understand the anxieties of the youth and speaks with the smugness of accomplishment, even though the adult may have undergone similar anxieties twenty or thirty years earlier. The adult is unable to communicate the feelings recalled over a distance of thirty years, the similar problems of his youth; but even if he succeeds in communicating, the very fact of his apparent success in life diminishes the impact of these anxieties.

Therefore, no matter how understanding, the adult seems to the youth, he sounds like a Boy Scout leader. The only understanding audience is a band of brothers, a peer group who are roughly the same age, composed of those who are undergoing roughly the same problems and are pretty much in the same stage of development. Only they can provide mutual support, the sharing of anxiety, and the sympathy based on an immediately felt common problem. Peer culture is a continuous set of common steps in the process of individuation.

While part of the culture of peer groups is the sharing of grievances in the process of self-realization, the goals of achievement that are the private aspirations of each individual in the shared culture make the transcending of grievances the object of the culture. The peer culture in these circumstances appears to be an objective, collective, socially organized culture which has strong sanctions and pressures for conformity to its standards, including the necessity of maintaining the secrets of the group in opposition to the standards of others. At the same time the peer group and its culture operate to assure and support the *individual* in his quest for the achievement of *individual* skills and competence at a time when he is most uncertain of those skills. The latent goals may be the achievement of the individual goals of its respective members, and the social collective goals and culture are only incidental to this task. In this sense, when the individual achieves his purposes in the group, he may graduate to other groups that use similar methods to achieve other, more advanced purposes or may become an individual not needing group support. He may join other kinds of peer groups that have less instrumental purposes. In the last case, the new peer group may exist simply to enjoy common interests, sensibility, friendship.

Mobility-oriented Peer Groups

The totally successful and the total failures each drop out of their respective mobility-oriented peer cultures when they achieve their social destinies. Each may, however, join a peer culture that corresponds to his arrival. But the vicissitudes of achievement, of mobility, of failure and success are so varied, both in total and at each age level, that the self-selection of the individual for participation in particular peer groups and cultures appears to be almost unlimited, and the variety of peer cultures is also unlimited.

These mobility and compliance-oriented peer cultures serve as sources of support, as sounding boards for individuals whose private goals are of greater value to them than the value of the peer culture itself; that is, the goal is to transcend the peer culture, which serves only as a momentary depository for the releasing of anxieties and insecurities arising in the process of attempting to achieve social and technical facility and success. The goal is thus always individual, and the peer group is a temporary alliance of individuals pursuing similar goals. Given these limitations, the levels of intimacy are likely to be much narrower than among peer groups formed at earlier ages. The peers in such groups are less likely to reveal aspects of themselves that suggest incapacity for ultimate achievement of their common but separate goals. And the anxieties and grievances so revealed in their common culture ought not to be present in stark terms that suggest that the individual seems unlikely to keep up with his peers. Moreover, the individual risks endangering the group by presenting, in his grievances and compliants, an image of the impossibility of success; he risks dampening, by sympathetic communication, the aspirations, resolves, or discipline of the others. These others, from the standpoint of their own aspirations, are not inclined to accept or support others whose intimacy is a drag on their own aspirations. Thus, such peer groups and the individuals in them at times appear to be cruel to each other and to the group. From the standpoint of their own sense of self, peer group members are cruel to each other and to the group when such cruelty is necessary to maintain their original individual aspirations. They may exclude from their group those whose failures are greater than the average of the group or those who do not keep up with the average success of the group; or they may so condescend to such failures as to make group membership intolerable to the less successful. At the same time, conspicuous success may induce the successful to seek membership in new groups whose aspirations and success match his own, perhaps recent, achievement. He may become unbearable in his original group because of crowing or condescension, or because others feel that he is. Such departures from peer groups are likely to be celebrated in distant alumni gatherings, where the respective members can celebrate their common problems and their relative success, and one of the functions of the alumni meeting is to provide the basis for a final calculation of relative mobility and success, a calculation that is likely to be incomplete, because the least successful are likely to disappear from the social horizons of the group; only the most successful are likely to show up. The limited character of such mobility-oriented peer groups means that the same fullness of self-revelation, depth of intimacy, and absence of a sense of embarrassment at intimacy are all less developed than in more youthful peer groups oriented to simply dealing with the fact of puberty and sexual exploration itself.[9] After all, the problems of puberty and sexuality are far more universal than the separate avenues and experience of social, occupational, and economic mobility.

Friendship and the Life Cycle

Because friendship is so variable in its nature and forms, one can only attempt to specify some of the social matrices within which friendship typically emerges.

The friendships of preadolescents are likely to be naive and unreflective, largely because the boundaries of the self and of friends are not clearly drawn. One does not know when one is being too intimate or too stand-offish, because one is too self-centered. The principal concern is with expressing and articulating the self rather than dealing with the other. In their naivete these preadolescent friendships may reflect the parental class and ethnic differences, parental attitudes to authority, and differences in parental attitudes that are unreflectively absorbed by the friends. They of course reflect propinquity, interest, and the personal characteristics of the individuals in question.

Adolescent Friendship

In adolescence, when the individual becomes more aware of his separateness from parents, from siblings, and even from his peers, the individual attempts to establish boundaries for himself and to become a unique self, to discover his own tastes and preferences, and to shape his future; then all the contradictions and conflicts between past and an emerging future are heightened. The individual no longer is willing to accept—at least unreflectively—all of the forces, influences, and pressures that have operated on him. But he usually does not know the directions he ultimately will choose. Usually the range of options, at least in imagination, are greater than he can choose from, and his full potentialities—in the absence of testing—are unknown to him. In this "anomie of adolescence," friendship is a means of making tentative choices, in the sense that common but restricted interests become a path toward the future. Moreover, the intimacy of friendship becomes the means by which the adolescent finds in the other a sounding board upon which to project his own uncertainties, his explorations and defeats, his grievances and victories before others who are sufficiently in the same situation as to understand these explorations without being condescending or, in times of doubt, overly affirmative. The friendships that arise in this period tend to be deeper and longer-lasting than all other friendships. They can and usually do serve as a reference point for the total subsequent life of the individual, regardless of changes in career, in life history, in relative success and failure. These friendships become a stable point of reference, at times equal to those provided by the family, in the total life of an individual.

Friendships that emerge in later stages of one's life tend to be of a more limited character; they may be based on common place of residence, place of work, common social activities, career patterns, and emerging common interests. Even among these, of course, the possibility emerges that particular friendships will broaden and deepen to the point that they become intimate friendships. Yet the governing situation is that, in the main part of one's adult life, two other sets of commitments are dominant: commitment to career and commitment to family.

Commitments to career mean, quite frequently, changes of residence; but more to this point is the investment of the major energies of the striver in his work and to the demands of work. Friendships, of course, occur, those of convenience at work and those maintained in relaxation from work. But so long as work becomes the major axis upon which a life is built, friendship is usually sacrificed to the demands of work.

Friendship, Marriage, and the Family

At least in the early life of the young married couple, the emotional demands of the family are paramount in several respects. First of all, just the depth of an intimate relationship may lead the individuals in question to avoid the expenditure of psychic energy in nonfamily relationships, or at least to limit such expenditures. The couple may face the problem of reconciling the demands of premarital friendships on other, more limited bases than those expressed in the marriage. The premarital friendship may be reconstituted on more limited bases than those expressed in the marriage. For example, a premarital friendship based on the husband's love of nature may be restricted by the wife's hatred of nature. Marriage usually results in a reassortment, a reevaluation, and a differential alignment of the strength of friendship after marriage. Some friendships become so attenuated that they may cease to exist, and others develop a different balance of strength. A husband may continue friendships that are not shared with the wife, but to the extent that the common activities of the marriage are central, these friendships become peripheral.

Part of the adjustment of marriage is in dealing with the kind of constraints and demands placed upon a marriage by the acquisition of new sets of in-laws. We are not here concerned primarily with the troubles and tension that in-law strife and competition bring. We focus more on the fact that social obligations involving in-laws place a time limit on the social obligations involving premarital friends. One simply has less time for one's old friends. When limits on career and social mobility are reached, and when a husband or father, on the basis of these limits, no longer feels obligated to invest most of his psychic life in work, he may have more time available to give to either friends or family. The friendships so developed are likely to be friendships of residential propinquity or of relaxation outside of work, and limited friendships based on resistance to the demands of work within his place of work.

In addition, the creation of a family as an institution, with its common tasks of making a home, bearing and raising children, preoccupation with the common family activities, home furnishing, and supervising the education, the extracurricular activities, and the problems of children, all become central. New friendships emerge, focused upon commitment to these family-centered activities. Young singles, young adults, young parents, and so forth become the pool from which new friends are drawn within the boundaries of propinquity, personal taste, personal styles, socialibility, income, religion, and so forth. Again, since the framework of friendship is based on objective aspects of the life cycle, they tend to be more limited, though not necessarily less satisfying. Moreover, to repeat, any friendship can break through the limits of a friendship of convenience or propinquity. One can merely say in summary that in these young adult and middle years the constraints of the external world are such as to limit the possibility of such breakthroughs.

Friendship and Maturity

A final limit on the friendship of maturity may be suggested here. Friendships in the middle years, especially in the middle classes, tend to be based on the exhibition of arrival, on achievements, whether those achievements are real or imaginary. The individual is expected to project, in his total way of life, his status as a mature adult. At this stage he usually avoids projecting images of weakness, of failure, or of the foibles associated with youth and adolescence. Such images are inappropriate to one's age. But they are part of every man's human condition. Therefore, the mature individual usually projects to new friends an image of the self that denies to others access to his private or intimate self. At the same time his experience, accomplishments, and background, his achieved levels of taste and forms of expertise allow him to project, with some degree of ease and poise, aspects of the self which make for a limited sociability and personal interchange reflecting his levels of accomplishment. Thus, friendship develops and can provide most of the needs for sociability and for cultural, social, or recreational interests and provides the background for both a nonfamily and non-work-related social and home life. Such friendships are intrinsically different from the friendships of adolescence and youth and from the more situationally determined friendships of early marriage. At the same time these friendships may coexist with friendships that survive from adolescence, youth, and younger adulthood. Simply because they are an added level to all of these, and to the level of commitments entailed in one's family position, they are not expected to be as broad or as deep. They provide comfort.

Intimacy and Personal Crises

All of this means that intimacy is not an expectation of such friendship of maturity. Of course, such friendships may devolve into intimacy. The requirement that the friendship of maturity serve as a device for projecting one's mature arrival precludes the projection of elements of failure and youthful "immaturity" that are the signs of a common humanity. Such projections of maturity are based in part upon arrival. The fact of failure—a divorce or a bankruptcy, unemployment, arrest, or exposure for violation of law or of sanctioned norms—strains the quality of the limitation placed on such friendships. Those whose friendships are based on the limited nature of the relationship may now find that the new situation of failure places a demand on them to respond at deeper levels than found in the original relationship or to move, because of the exposure to deeper levels of humanity, to a more intimate relationship. The cost of achieving the new basis for relationships may become too great. Too much is demanded of the friend. In such a situation, the individual in crisis may find that his friends are not "true friends" and may feel deserted. When this occurs, he usually is unable to recognize that his prior friendship did not entail the deeper relationship of commitment and intimacy that he avoided until the crisis. On the other hand, some partners in limited friendships may come to the support of their all-too-human friend. In part, the situation of crisis provides an opportunity to achieve at least a temporary intimacy, ordinarily denied in success.

Moreover, the crisis situation will tend to reveal aspects of the self that are usually denied in situations of success. The crisis-bound individual may lack the capacity to maintain the defenses that prevent or limit his intimacy. In revealing himself as all-too-human, he makes himself available to those who need to share in his or their joint humanity. He thus makes himself available for intimacy, the intimacy of crisis. Moreover, if the crisis is asymmetrical, he makes himself available, quite often, to the well-meant condenscension and sense of superiority implicit in asymmetrical relationships. This kind of one-sided response to one's enforced intimacy may be more difficult to bear than the estrangement of a limited, distant equality.

The crisis situation provides the opportunity for the "sociable strangers" of a limited friendship to reveal those aspects of the self which they previously had not projected because of the limited nature of their social contract. Thus, the crisis-bound person discovers that all or a great many of his mature friends now, because of his crisis, project to him reports of their own corresponding crises, of human derelictions and deformities that they had previously concealed because of the limited nature of their prior friendship and sociability. Thus, the individual in crisis discovers a previous culture, a "democracy," of crisis situations, which surround him and of which to a large degree he was previously unaware. He is given psychological and emotional support, which, however, is more likely to help him sink than swim, because at the moment of distress he may be bearing the weight of everybody else's past submergence; or he may, on the contrary, discover that if they could float and weather the storm, perhaps he can.

The limited friendships of adulthood, when not subject to crisis, are not necessarily based on ignorance or the inability to imagine the humanity and the intimacy that much inevitably lie behind the projection of the limited values in the social relationship. But the original "agreement" to limit the social relationship within the parameters of maturity and success means that there is an implicit agreement to avoid probing, to avoid revealing one's self, and to avoid broadening and deepening the relationship. Tact, the avoidance of the invasion of privacy, is characteristic of such limited intimacy. This delicacy of feeling, knowing when to reveal the self and when not to ask questions, becomes an essential quality of all limited friendships. What it means, of course, is that friendship is not necessarily connected with intimacy. And to the extent that intimacy is involved, it is far more voluntaristic than the intimacy that is imposed upon individuals by the fact of marriage, by the fact of biological intimacy, and by the compulsory aspects of the sexual and marital relationship. The ability to achieve a psychological intimacy in the absence of a physical intimacy and to maintain such a relationship with tact and a respect for the other is far more difficult to achieve and to maintain.

The Friendship of Old Age

One reason for the limited nature of mature adult friendship is the necessity that mature adults have of projecting images of their own arrival, success, and maturity. They feel that they cannot afford to allow their failures, their common biological humanity—these ingredients of deep intimacy—to interfere with their projection of mature success. They are too much in a public world to allow the privacy of self to interfere with that projection of their place in the public world. Old age alters this perspective. Upon retirement, upon withdrawal from the public world, and upon a sense of having achieved and then withdrawn, the requirements to defend the self against public values are slackened. The elderly person can afford to admit the failures of youth and middle age. He has nothing more to defend or to lose. He can enjoy retailing and retelling the frauds he committed as part of his public presentation. He can admit the crimes that he will no longer be punished for. And he feels that telling the truth is now permissible. At this point in his life he can make public the intimate; but at this point in his life his public self-exposure is not treated as seriously, since he has nothing to lose but his past. As a result, a new level of more intimate exposure or self-projection emerges among the elderly. And this retailing of the triumphs and defeats of one's past public and intimate self can be the basis of new kinds of intimate friendships. These friendships may cut across age lines or may be the basis of age-graded peer friendships. Across age lines, the oldster may profit from the opportunity of telling the truth, when the younger person, at virtually any age level, being still in the competitive struggle, must protect his intimate self from exposure. The oldster may teach the "facts of life," the realities of the relationship between public and private behavior, to those who may need to know but are constrained from having to admit or reveal both their ignorance and their knowledge. And this may be true, no matter how many outrageous lies the oldster may tell in dramatizing his earlier life, accomplishments, and defalcations. This educational function is important, since it allows for the presentation of quasi-public behavior, of a sense of the interpenetration between public and private life in social situations. This is possible, again, only because the elder has nothing to lose by his self-revelation. He can even dramatize himself by so doing.

Of course, at the older ages of senescence and senility, the dependence of the elder becomes manifest to the younger and approaches the dependence that an infant or child has on his elders. The inability to protect one's sense of privacy can become the basis of an enforced asymmetrical intimacy.

The other case of old-age intimacy is the intimacy of age-graded peers. Here, too, the absence of a need for defenses caused by not having to attempt to control or influence the public world allows for the expression of the self in ways that are not generally permissible among mature adults and even in youthful friendship relationships. Again, the mutual boasting and revelation of sins and defalcations of one's youth become part of the public aspects of old-age culture and of the friendships that take place within that culture. Because they are part of that culture, they are not particularly intimate in such situations, where tolerance, affection, and trust are necessary ingredients to the relationship. The aged individual grants very little when he grants intimacy, and receives very little of value when it is returned in kind. The individual earns by his age, and by the weakening of his defenses, the right to act out the private and the intimate in public, in almost the same way as does the infant. And he warrants, on the basis of old age, the kind of tolerance that a child or infant necessarily demands. It is both a concession to and a strain on those youngsters, the mature children of the old-aged, who, because of their own limited situation, feel the necessity to retain boundaries between the private self and public projection. The children must grant, out of respect, necessity, or affection, that degree of tolerance which they cannot grant to themselves, except in situations of deep intimacy. And this degree of respect is the price that those in the struggle to remain in the mainstream, must grant to those who are out of it.

Notes

1. See, in Ernest Hemingway's *The Sun Also Rises,* the portrayal of Cohn.

2. George Herbert Mead, *Mind, Self and Society,* ed. Charles W. Morris (Chicago, University of Chicago Press, 1934), pp. 317–18: "The adult finds it difficult, to say the least, to put himself into the attitude of the child. That is not, however, an impossible thing." See also pp. 149–51.

3. S. Freud, *Civilization and Its Discontents,* trans. and ed. James Strachey (New York: Norton, 1962), pp. 76–78.

4. See Mead, *Mind, Self, and Society, loc, cit., Civilization and Its Discontents, loc. cit.*

5. Relevant to this entire discussion is an article by Arnold W. Green, "The Middle-Class Male Child and Neurosis," *American Sociological Review,* February 1946, pp. 31–41, reprinted in Logan Wilson and William L. Kolb, eds., *Sociological Analysis* (New York: Harcourt, Brace, 1949), pp. 236–47. On p. 247 of Wilson and Kolb: ". . . the most characteristic neurosis of modern society—per-

sonality absorption," of which the major components are "the reiterated threat to withdraw a love which has been made of paramount importance" and "a conflict between the resulting initial adjustment of submissive propitiation and the later assumption of goals of achievements and roles of independent action."

6. J. H. van den Berg, "Adults and Children" (chapter 2), in *The Changing Nature of Man: Introduction to a Historical Psychology*, trans. from the Dutch by H. F. Croes (New York: Norton, 1961; Delta reprint, 1975), p. 29: "Campe's Complaint" to the effect that it was not at all pleasurable to see eight- or ten-year-olds discoursing like adults—a complaint that emerged in Rousseau's day, according to van den Berg.

7. Allen Wheelis, *The Quest for Identity* (New York: W. W. Norton, 1958), pp. 126–27: "Formerly morality was obedience to the verities instilled by parents; it is coming now to be compliance with the practices of one's peers. . . . The site of the moral standard has also changed. The group has gained in authority at the expense of the conscience."

8. Erik H. Erikson, "Adolescence," in *Identity: Youth and Crisis* (New York: W. W. Norton, 1968), pp. 128–29.

9. For some portrayals of such groups, see novels such as J. P. Marquand, *The Late George Apley;* Ignazio Silone, *The Seed Beneath the Snow;* Mary McCarthy, *The Group,* and Jean Dutourd, *The Springtime of Life.*

Chapter 6

Intimacy as the Basis of Social Networks and Culture

In the discussion of friendship, especially of friendships of adults that cross the gradient of success, we have indicated that much of culture consists of the interchange of information based on intimate knowledge derived from friendships that becomes part of an informal culture as it is transmitted by interpersonal exchange (gossip). That discussion requires further elaboration.

We have indicated that friendship at any level of depth requires deep levels of trust. The friend or, for that matter, any intimate other is willing to reveal to a friend levels of information about himself that he trusts will not be used against him, which will be reciprocated by the exchange of similar complementary information. Friendship thus requires a compact of secrecy. This would appear to be clear in a dyadic relationship, i.e., if only two people are involved. The fly in the ointment is that any individual may have more than one friend. The expectation that one reveals a great deal of oneself in a friendship situation includes the notion that one reveals a great deal of the information that one derives from one friend or set of friends to another friend or set of friends; that is, friend B may be told information derived from one's friendship with friend A. To withhold information from friend B may violate the agreement to sus-

147

pend the withholding of information that constitutes much of friendship. But to reveal to friend B the information derived from friend A may violate the agreement to maintain the confidentiality of friendship which is the basis of the friendship with friend A. Thus there is an inherent contradiction in the very nature of friendship. Friendship implies both the sharing of information, of secrets, and the withholding of such information. The sharing of information is not only a *desideratum* of friendship, it is a necessity. It is a necessity because friends use their friendship to unburden themselves of secrets that they hold within themselves, a burden that ordinarily causes a sense of isolation from the public and official culture, which rejects the kinds of thoughts, actions, or information contained in the secret. Revealing the secret, then, is a release from the pressure of public opinion. But the demand for intimacy is based on the necessity and the opportunity to reveal such situations with the understanding that the other will not reveal such information to still others. In network friendships, the person who is the holder of the secret shifts; with each interchange of information, the necessity to both reveal and withhold shifts, along with the shift in information. The information that so circulates in a network is called "gossip," though one would have to distinguish the gossip of intimate information exchanged within a network or circle of close friends and the random aimless speculations about distant outsiders that is revealed in the mass media. In the latter case, the aimless gossip is a projection into mass-media-derived information, or the meanings one attributes on the basis of analysis derived from personal interchanges, whether or not these meanings may be true. When we deal with the interchange of gossip among a network of friends, the gossip has different meanings among different friends, and different functions. In a friendship or an intimate circle, if the various friends are friendly to each other (e.g., if friend A and friend B are friendly, so that a third friend reports of the activities of friend A to friend B), the gossip in question is "news." It creates a culture for a friendship circle or network; it sustains the entire circle. It is a kind of quasi-public information in a relatively intimate network or group. This quasi-public culture is essentially different from public or official culture. It contains elements of information that, if present in official culture—e.g., the newspapers, a court, a congressional investigating committee—would result in public prosecution, public scandals, the loss of prestige, and disgrace. If presented in an informal network, they constitute the juicy tidbits of dramatic incident which feed a friendship circle and which dramatize and prove one's membership in that circle. But since networks, through a series of one-to-one linkages, are almost infinite in length, the culture that is exchanged in such circles may have a very wide circulation. At a distance from the original two or three friends who exchange the primary confidences, the information may be distorted, may lose the details that guarantee its authenticity, or may be overelaborated by dramatic invention to make it appear to be improbable or impossible. At the peripheries, then, intimate gossip becomes baseless rumor. At the level of primary friendships the same "gossip" becomes a life-and-death secret which confirms a friendship and enables an individual to escape the burdens of privacy.[1]

The Intimate as Quasi-Public

Yet, because such information is diffused through extended networks, the culture so created contains secrets; violation of public norms; and reports of immoral, criminal, antisocial, or unconventional behavior as defined by the standards of the official public norms. Because the information so exchanged is quasi-private and quasi-public, the informal culture so presented is always at odds with the public, "official" culture. At any point in the social structure there tend to be two cultures: (1) a public, official culture, which expresses and sustains the public norms of a society, and (2) a quasi-public, quasi-private culture, which reveals the violation of the public, official norms and culture. In the words of F. G. Bailey: "No social world is even thinkable without the irresponsible circulation of information about persons." With respect to the public culture, almost every individual will have access to a vast amount of information concerning behavior that is immoral, illegal, and disgraceful. Loyalty to one's network or one's group implies not allowing such information to enter the official public world, where the rumors of such behavior or information would bring public action against the offending parties and those who cover up the information. Yet the uncontrolled flow of information through an endless series of network friendships and affiliations means that the quasi-public culture extends beyond those who have a strong loyalty to the principal subjects of the gossip. The extension of quasi-public culture into the social domain of the "enemies" of a network and to distant network members results in the possibility that quasi-public culture will

enter into official culture. The newspaper, the district attorney, or
the congressional investigator may seek to prosecute members of a
network for actions that were known in the quasi-public culture, by
means of an extended "gossip" network, for long periods of time.

The Conflict Between Quasi-Cultural and "Official" Culture

If and when this happens, a network may dissolve; suspicion is
engendered, and the actions that were tolerable within the network
become intolerable to the public. The original network includes, as
a "rule" or ethic, the norm of trust, of friendship, of respect for the
privacy and confidentiality of the friend. These friendship norms are
invoked to cover up the violation of public norms. At the same time,
each friend in such a network owes some degree of responsibility to
the public norms, to the legal code, and to the necessity of protecting himself against the possibility of prosecution or disgrace. Each
friend in such a situation has to make the decision as to whether to
spill the beans and save himself from extreme reprisals or to uphold
the norms friendship. At this point the decision becomes a personal
one; to violate the norms of friendship when overwhelming pressure
is *not* present is a betrayal of the norms of intimacy and friendship.
To insist on those norms when alternative evidence of the violation
of public standards is available is to incriminate onself; to insist on a
friend's maintenance of the norms of another friend's secrets at the
cost of incriminating oneself is to go beyond the norms of friendship.[2] Yet in each case the consequences of each alternative are not
clearly known in advance, so the decision to maintain public or
network norms is always ambiguous, fraught with deep anxiety and
the sense of betrayal of self, friend, or "the public."

The Network as a Basis for Society and Culture

We have looked at quasi-public culture from the standpoint of a
particular network.[3] We would have to recognize that in any complex society an uncountable number of such networks exist and that
the basis of such networks may vary. We have indicated that one

basis may be social class, though in a complex society any social class, no matter how defined, may include an uncountable number of such networks. In a small town class networks may be few in number and clearly recognizable.[4]

We have previously indicated that such network cultures can be defined as peer-group cultures in which age is the significant criterion for defining the peer group and the culture therein. Again, there may be an uncountable number of peer groups, all of which are smaller than the age classifications that become the outer perimeters of a given peer group.

Sex also may be the basis of peer cultures in which friends of the same sex exchange intimate information that is withheld from members of the opposite sex—wives, husbands, girlfriends, boyfriends, or age peers. Friendship networks may cut across each other; across age, sex, class, social and economic specialization, and so forth. Each network may withhold secrets from another even though some members of one network may be members of another network. But the fact that a network member may belong to more than one network, each network having a different basis, allows for the seepage of information through a number of networks. Because network members may experience loyalties of different strength to different networks, the confidential or secret information that members are privy to is not consistently or systematically maintained. Uneven rates of the diffusion of information through a plurality of networks becomes the basis of an interlacing of culture between the interlocking members of this plurality of networks. Such interlocks between networks also become an additional basis for the prevalence of rumor and distant gossip.

The totality of network gossip, as it seeps through a multitude of networks at uneven rates, constitutes the totality of the culture of a society, certainly of informal culture, of class, and of the information that makes up the framework of the life of most individuals in society. But because networks are relatively small, and because of the uneven distribution of information through an uncountable number of networks, there is relatively little uniformity and standardization of informal culture. Within smaller communities and smaller groups there are modalities, relatively clear-cut clusters of class, age, sex, and special interest and activity cultures, which become the basis of foci for "culture" in the abstract. But these modalities and core cultures are available primarily to insiders. At increasing distances they become abstract and distorted. To treat the modality as if it were the norm would be to overlook the vast range in culture based on levels of intimacy, friendship, size, peer group, cross-cutting of peer cultures, leakage, distortion, and both dilution or over-dramatization of the original information itself.

The sociologist or anthropologist, as he investigates culture at its primary levels, faces the problem of charting the topography of culture. He attempts to maintain the accuracy of his primary data (and thus gather information that is intimate, confidential, secret), and at the same time present it in relatively general terms so that outsiders can learn both the form and content of those cultures that are not readily available to themselves. Of course, each outsider to one quasi-public or network culture is an insider to other intimate, peer, and friendship cultures. The investigator risks the danger, in attempting to clarify the topography of culture, of making it abstract, unified, and uniform in content and form. In simplifying, he may, for the sake of economy, ignore the specific content that makes network culture unique to the participants involved—their personal and intimate needs, which gave rise to the culture in the first place. Moreover, if he simplifies to such an extent, he converts modalities into absolutes and fails to indicate the vast range and uneven distribution of the forms and content of culture.

Quasi-Culture and the Mass Media

The mass media, and in fact all public agencies concerned with the presentation of culture to wider audiences, necessarily diffuse intimate culture to audiences larger than the primary networks themselves. They do so for a variety of reasons. Some, in the interest of asserting the dominance of public norms (whatever their private interests may be), may publicize, through investigative reporting, the violation of public norms by intimate groups. In doing so they reassert the dominance of public standards over the particular standards of a particular network. For better or worse, they reassert the centrality of public official norms and prevent the dissolution of society into an uncountable number of network particularities.[5] In this way they maintain whatever uniformities there are to society as a whole. Other agencies of mass media, again for whatever reasons they may have, may report the immoral, illegal, and antisocial activities of particular networks in order to feed the striving for a sense of normality that all of us necessarily have as private individuals who are necessarily deviant from some dimensions of public culture. We have indicated that public, official culture always and necessarily represents less than (and more than) the potentiality of the private individual. In suggesting that others are in their own ways as deviant as we are or would like to be, they make our deviancy more normal than it would be if we were to face that deviancy in isolation. The report of the deviancy of others serves to normalize our own, though the normalizing of our own deviancy might, in its totality, devalue the public standards that constitute the basis of society.

The mass media, in performing both functions, reasserting the centrality of public norms and normalizing the prevalence of deviancy, have to contend with the fact that friendship networks are to all practical purposes infinite in number. They cannot present them all. In making a selection they necessarily distort the total number and the range of peer groups and their cultures, and thus necessarily misrepresent the culture and structure of a society as a whole. Generally they resolve the problem in two basic ways: In the first case, they will seek to represent the "deviant" intimate aspects of those networks and individuals who occupy public roles, and at the same time devalue our public heroes and assert their accountability to public norms. Second, they will search for those conspicuous examples of the violation of public norms that are so extreme that they both dramatize the public norm and exculpate the less serious offenders by overshadowing their offenses. A man biting a dog is news, but a man devouring a friend, a spouse, or his children would, by such a standard, be even more newsworthy.[6]

But as the dynamic of searching for extremes of deviancy results in the normalization through publicity of each incident or kind of deviancy, the quest for extremes may well result in the normalization of successive levels of deviancy to the point where we are satiated with deviancy. When that stage is reached, we may find that the mass media are forced to normalize public norms and normality. We may, after the normality of the counter-culture of the 1960s, have some distance to go before the normality of the 1950s becomes respectable. There are signs that this is occurring.

Conflicting Demands Between Public and Quasi-Public Moralities

We have indicated that a requirement of intimacy is trust and confidentiality, and that deep levels of intimacy result in the exchange of information that necessarily and optimally violates public norms. But we have also indicated that, when such exchanges occur, the fact that individuals have more than one friend and the requirements of intimacy result in the exchange of information along an extended serial network. When the friend of a friend is also the friend of another, the exchange of information among the three may result in an intimate culture and in gossip that may be reasonably accurate. But life unfortunately is not always that simple. Friend A may hate Friend B, and the information that I receive from Friend A, if I were to report it to Friend B, could result in Friend B's using it against Friend A. Friend B, in exchange for his confidence, may expect me to report not only my intimate behavior but also the intimate behavior of Friend A that I have learned in my relationship with Friend A. At the same time, since Friend A has burdened me with reports of his behavior, in assuming the burden of knowledge I have so learned I share the needs to unburden myself of that burden that Friend A has placed upon me.

In addition, of course, I may choose to either reciprocate with Friend B for the information that he has provided me by reporting the information that I have learned from Friend A. In addition, I may dramatize myself to either friend by reporting the information provided by that other. Yet in cases where I know that friend B may misuse the information provided to me by Friend A, I must withhold that information to prevent its misuse. The problems that ensue are twofold. One is that I do not know or may not learn of the misuse of such information until after the damage is done, or I may not learn that Friend A has learned of Friend B's abuse of information that Friend A provided to me until it is too late. "Too late" means that the damage has been done, and that I have lost one friend by responding to the demands of another friend. On the other hand, I may choose not to report to Friend B information that emerges out of my friendship with Friend A. If I refrain from so reporting, I may be violating the trust, the sense of intimacy with Friend B. In violating this norm, I may not know whether Friend B would in fact violate his friendship with me by reporting on what I told him. This inherent contradiction in the nature of the pluralities of friendship is, in principle, unresolvable. In practical terms it is resolved by the process of the gradual descent into friendship. Since friendships usually develop over long periods of time, the individual in question may be able to judge how a newfound friend handles the information that emerges from progressive deepening of friendship, and in the process decides at what level he will reveal himself and the information that he derives from other friendships. In this process he determines the level of intimacy that the new friendship will entail. And because of differing judgments friendships can occur at various levels of breadth and intimacy. Even this process is not as smooth or mechanical as our description implies. Friends of friends encounter each other at different levels of friendship than one encounters each with respect to oneself. Thus friends of friends may become friends of each other, and the level of intimacy of all three may be deepened, but friends of friends may become enemies because of factors that may not be related to one's own friendship with each. The level of one's reporting of intimate behavior of one to another may alter on the basis of the external relationship of each to another. Previously acceptable reporting may become no longer acceptable; one may have to alter the degree of trust and confidentiality of such reporting as a result of these external relations. Yet each friend may expect the third party to retain the previous level of intimacy. Altering the previous level may be seen as "taking sides," becoming less friendly, and "lining up" against him. Such disruptions in friendship patterns occur most frequently and drastically in divorce cases, where one is expected either to break off with one of the divorced couple or to become increasingly tactful or distant in the quality of one's relationship with one of the divorced or separated pair. Regardless of what one does, the relationship of friendship is altered, as well as the level of intimacy. The third party in question, moreover, cannot always assess the response of the others and risks losing a friendship as a consequence of betraying either or both friendships in maintaining the same levels of intimacy that previously had been stabilized among the three parties in question. The course of true friendship is rarely smooth; such perils are the natural risks that one undertakes in the course of friendship. The perils are minimized by sensitivity, tact, and the awareness of the consequence of one's actions, but employing such tact suddenly at times consists of the weakening of the intimacy of friendship.

The Burdens of Intimacy

Our discussion of friendship as a particular form of intimacy, a form that permits various levels of intimacy, has turned in part upon the conversion of the content of intimate social relations into culture. It is also focused on the moral dilemmas faced by a friend or intimate in dealing with other friends and intimates and with public, official norms and standards. Another factor that one must consider is the burdens of intimacy and friendship, burdens that may be perceived as a limiting cost of entry into friendship and intimate relations and, after entry, may limit the depth or progress into depth of intimacy.

We indicated the burdens of privacy, noting that pure privacy may emerge out of the necessities or the inabilities to comply totally with public and official norms that fail to express the totality of the individual. Privacy may emerge out of the physiological makeup of the individual, out of his psychological response to the attempt to socialize him into publicly acceptable behavior, out of his or her response to the perceived threat to the self by hostile agencies of socialization, and out of the fact that at any given moment the individual may be at odds with the immediately perceived public standards of behavior. From this point of view intimacy is shared privacy. Intimate behavior involves the willingness of individuals to express aspects of themselves to intimate others who are willing to tolerate and accept behavior that is not accepted, not tolerated, or frowned upon in public or official circles. In exchange for such acceptance by an intimate other, the individual is asked to accept the revelation of similar behavior on the part of the other. Since the parties in question, initially strangers, necessarily start from the public level, the process of becoming intimate is usually a slow and gradual one in which confidences and images of one's private self are revealed progressively at deeper and deeper levels. But the process is fraught with danger. Each individual, no matter how intimate he may become, is, to the extent that he is not psychotic, a public or social character. That is, he internalizes public and social roles that are at odds, again necessarily, with the roles he assumes as an intimate other. The process of becoming intimate is thus a process of the progressive abandonment of public or social roles. Yet at any stage the process of revealing the intimate, the deviant, the violation of public roles by one party may offend the other, either because of differences in tastes for self-revelation or in the revelation of an aspect of the private self that does not correspond to the content of the other's rejection of the public role. That which I reveal may be morally intolerable to you. Beyond this, the willingness to accept the discarding of public stances and the projection of images of a private, unsocial self involves the willingness to trust the other in his acceptance of one's own forms of deviant privacy and to trust the other's acceptance of oneself. This is usually conditioned by love, friendship, or deep affection. When such conditions appear to be absent, an asymmetric relation may emerge, wherein the self-revelation, or the need for self-revelation, by one party may constitute an opportunity for the exploitation of the other by that party. Thus, intimate relations consist in the attempt to escape the burdens of privacy by finding social supports for a private, intimate self that are short of the demands of public and official norms. One escapes the burden of privacy, but one undertakes the burdens of intimacy.

The question remains: What are the burdens of intimacy? These can be classified in two dimensions: the burdens that one wishes to impose on another, and the burdens that one assumes from another. The burdens that one wishes to impose on another entail an estimate of the willingness of the other to reveal reciprocally aspects of himself, when the individual has no way of knowing in advance whether or not the other will accept the burden. The burden that is to be imposed on the other is weighed in relation to the burden of privacy. If I am isolated, if I am deviant in ways that I feel to be extreme, I may be under great pressure to share my burden, even though the other with whom I would share it with is under no pressure to accept my burden. If I am a homosexual or a criminal, affected by guilt, I may confess to someone whom I regard as a friend, only to discover that my confession evokes horror and the termination of friendship. If the pressure to confess is great, and my knowledge of the possible response of the other is uncertain, the pressure to share the burden of privacy is an added pressure to that of the burden of privacy alone. I may teeter on the threshold of confession for a substantial part of my life until I risk rejection or until I become sure of acceptance. If I do neither, and retain this aspect of my privacy, I may remain a permanent stranger to my friend. I may maintain a friendship of limited liabilities, a friendship with minimal intimacy. To the extent to which this is a general condition of all my social relations, I will be a marginal man. Perhaps I may discover relationships of various degrees of intimacy with various others, so that I have distributed the burdens of privacy among a range of others such that I no longer have the overwhelming need for intimacy with many others and can accept relatively casual friendships and acquaintances. But in most of my social relationships I will be partially estranged from my friends and intimates, and in this sense some alienation is a condition of friendship.

The need for overcoming the burdens of privacy by creating the burdens of intimacy becomes paramount only when no genuine possibility for intimacy exists. The presence of only a few genuine intimate relations obviates the powerful pressures for intimacy and the need to weary casual friends and acquaintances with burdens they are unwilling to share or assume, or burdens that one does not know that they are willing to share. Moreover, such genuine intimacy prevents one's manipulation by others in asymmetric intimacies in which the other does not in fact share burden of intimacy.

The burdening of another with one's private self may be fraught with deep anxiety, but the burdens of accepting another's intimate self may be far more complex. Thus, the confession, the sense of having to share the weight of another's privacy, always presupposes one's willingness to make an equivalent confession. If one has no such need, then the task of carrying the load of the other provides no compensation other than the sense of power one may have in appearing to be so strong.

Carrying another's burden in the sense meant above means a willingness to enter a set of social relations that rest upon one's revealing one's self. One may not want to do 80 because of the lack of any particular nced to do so. This lack of need may be based on the fact that one already has a series of intimate relations that provide for a sharing of one's weight of privacy, or that one's sense of isolation from the public norms is not that great a burden. One may suspect, in addition, that in opening the gates to further confession by another, one may discover those forms of deviancy that are particularly abhorrent or distasteful to oneself regardless of the fact that one may wish to express one's own form of deviancy. Moreover, in accepting the invitation to express the content of one's own intimate or deviant behavior, one may be asked to reveal those aspects of oneself which one knows that the other may not accept. To avoid confession, one feels one must not accept confession. Finally, in this vein, the reciprocation of intimacy involves placing onself in the hands of another. In responding by confession to the confession of another, one places one's trust in the other, but the fact that another may trust me does not mean I need to trust him. To avoid the reproach of not being trusting, and to avoid placing my trust in one whom I am not sure is trustworthy, I may express unwillingness to accept his or her confession. In doing so, I limit the possibility of a deeper friendship, a more intimate social relationship. In the same sense, if I accept the confession of another and thus imply a willingness to make my own reciprocal confessions, I imply either deeper love, affection, and friendship that the fact of accepting a confession seems to imply on the face of it. Limited acceptance of intimate information is thus a denial of deeper friendship or of deeper commitment.

At another level still, acceptance of intimacy means a willingness to share the emotional anguish, the anxiety, the problems that confession entails. I may choose to do so on a number of grounds. First, I may be willing to accept another's troubles in exchange for acceptance of my own—that is, our friendship consists in pooling our troubles in the hope that, because of the different saliencies of our respective troubles, each individual can find the weight of each other's troubles easier to bear than the weight of the troubles he or she bears separately. Each of us, in lightening our own heavy load, and adopting a lighter load, may have in total a lighter load than the combined weight of our separate troubles. This calculus may be true, because, in the final analysis, one's private troubles may always be the heaviest.

In established friendships and intimacies, the commitment of the past may entail a progressive sharing of the burdens of another or the redistribution of the weights of those burdens. Love, friendship, or deep affection means that sudden misfortune, new problems, or the unusual course of the distribution of good and bad fortune may mean that one party to a deeply intimate relation has an increased need to share his troubles and that, simply because one has been involved in that relationship, one has shared one's burdens with the other. One cannot refuse—one may not even think of refusing—the new burdens. This, after all, is the ultimate meaning of love, friendship, and deep affection.

But in the final analysis in accepting the burdens of another, one is accepting the responsibility for distributing one's emotional resources, one's capacity for love, affection, and friendship, among a plurality of others. Different individuals have different capacities for love or friendship, and different capacities to distribute friendship among a plurality of others. We can say that some people are capable only of loving themselves; whether this in fact is true may be open to question. But the statement does suggest that they have limited capacities for loving others. For some, the affectual range may include only members of our immediate family to which some sense of possession is attached, while others may be able to extend their range only to old friends, and they may find it difficult to enter new friendships or may do so only over extended periods of time. But, whatever the affectual capacity of an individual may be, each new friendship, each new level of intimacy, may cause a redistribution of affectual ties among a plurality of individuals. An individual with a great capacity for friendship may find that this very talent may constitute an invitation for those in pressing need for intimacy to overburden another whose very capacity has caused him to be already overburdened. The capacity for intimacy, one's sociability, one's openness, one's inner resources, all are an invitation to be profligate with those resources until the individual in question learns that new friendships, new intimacies, constitute a basis, desired or not, for thinning out and losing established friendships and intimacies. If the individual is initially nonreflective, he may discover that he has lost old friends who are not a burden in the process of acquiring new and burdensome friends. If he becomes reflective in the process of discovering what he has done, he may decide to limit himself in accepting new burdens and thus refuse to entertain the confessions of others or to reciprocate in those confessions. The seeming indifference to the entry into new levels of intimacy by people who seem to have the capacity for doing so may be an attempt to limit the emotional demands upon oneself or to preserve the intimate social relations one already has. Such behavior may seem inexplicable to the person whose burden of privacy is great and needs to lighten it by sharing his other burden of intimacy with whomever he can.

Of course, this discussion of the affectually rich person, who, by virtue of his richness, becomes the object of continuous borrowings and beggings, applies only to the rich. Others, of more limited resources, may not have such problems, and the confession of such problems are not easily shared.

Given the inequality of affectual ranges, the problem of sharing the burdens of intimacy is not easily resolvable. There is no legislative way of sharing this wealth. Individuals in need may discover that their greatest sacrifices of self and revealing of self to another may be viewed as sacrifices even though, in the sacrifice that relieves oneself of the burden of privacy, the burdens are not accepted. And those who do not or cannot accept the burden of others because they are already overloaded, given their affectual range, quite often cannot understand, when they reject the gestures of intimacy of others, why their rejection elicits bitterness. The sense of mutual estrangement is not likely to be shared.

The burdens of intimacy are most easily shared when the parties to a would-be intimate relationship are in equal need of, and have equal resources for, intimacy. But the exigencies of private life, personal development, and opportunity are not equally available to all. The inequality in personal and private development and resources constitutes an inevitable set of inequalities that make the possibility of sharing the loads of intimacy fragile.*

Intimacy and Exclusion

One of the uses, or perhaps we should say abuses, of intimacy or the idea of intimacy is the use of intimate discussion, gestures, and references to exclude third parties.[7] Two or more persons in a larger group, who, having established on the basis of their past a set of intimate references, may quite consciously steer the conversation into areas where the outsiders cannot participate or are embarrassed to, or they speak on subjects in which the outsiders cannot, or would refuse to participate. The range of topics implies minimally exclusion and maximally offensiveness. In between lies the embarrassing of the outsider. In some cases one party may be excessively or demonstratively affectionate to another in order to demonstrate possessiveness or a special relationship, or to provoke jealousy in the third party. Such demonstrations of affection are likely to be provocative when in fact no affection is present. The appearance of the third party may elicit demonstrations of affection for the duration of the presence, or for the initial stages of the presence of the third party, and disappear either when the third party leaves or when the affectionate ones become habituated to the presence of the third party. In either case the

*Given the needs for confession of deviancy and private rejection or inability to comply with public social codes, combined with unequal distribution of possibilities for confession, there arises the opportunity and need for impersonal confession. The Church confessional may release individuals of the burden of guilt and deviancy which apparently a friend or intimate cannot provide. A psychiatrist, and in our era the medical doctor, may in a secular age do the same thing, for which they are well paid. Confessing to total strangers whom one is not likely to see again may provide a temporary release which need never be repeated and is therefore less effective. Confessing to a judge, a policeman, or a district attorney may result in the unburdening of guilt, sometimes for crimes that were not committed, though if committed, the release of guilt is likely to bring about new kinds of social relations and new forms of intimacy. Confession in the mass media, after one has presumably been punished according to law, may result in fame and fortune if the crime was big enough, dramatic enough, or celebrated. These confessions, however, are more likely to produce material benefits at the expense of deeper personal gratification. If the individual, however, has been punished, or feels he has punished himself in the legal process, the gains from the subsequent public confession may be simply extra benefits, though they serve to confirm one's sense of delinquency together with one's sense of celebrity.

appearances of intimacy may be difficult to sustain. The object of the affection and pseudo-intimacy may feel misused or abused, or used as an object, but subject to a hidden scenario which he may only dimly realize. Much of such playing at intimacy is related to the dynamics of courtship and sexual games. In part it may be done to freeze out potential opposition by demonstrating a false claim on the affection of others, or it may be done to demonstrate a trophy in the struggle for affection and intimacy. Finally, such behavior may be pure sadism designed to wound either the object of the claim for intimacy or the witness, who is viewed, perhaps, as having a prior claim and whose claim is now denied by the pseudo-claim.

Not all public demonstrations of intimacy in nonintimate situations are necessarily so self-conscious or geared to such diabolical inventions. In many cases a simple history of long-established, deeply personal intimate relations establishes frameworks of references, understandings, and meanings, whose very presence results in the fact that third parties become outsiders. At times the outsider must necessarily feel his "alienation" from the intimate group. Given the fact that the outsider, in his own personal relations, has similar patterns of intimacy that necessarily exclude outsiders, he will take for granted the fact that in many groups he must necessarily be treated as an outsider. This is likely to cause little strain, unless the outsider feels that he has no intimate reference group anywhere, that he is always a stranger, and that individuals always treat him as an outsider. In the absence of his own resources for intimacy, such treatment is an act of provocation. Such exclusion is likely to result in heightened demands for inclusion in intimate groups when the prior basis for the creation of intimacy is absent. The individual may assert a claim for intimacy by becoming more intimate in his self-revelation, in order thereby to invite intimate responses and inclusion. If his motives for seeking intimacy are his immediate need and do not have a previously established basis, his assertion of claims to intimacy may be regarded as an unwarranted invasion of the privacy of others and rejected, despite the fact that those who reject him may display an easy intimacy among themselves. The outsider may feel that the denial of intimacy is an act of aggression against himself, that intimacy or gestures of intimacy as public behavior are a denial of human decency. At the same time, he may feel that intimacy should be democratized, made available to all at no or little social cost to those who would like to receive its benefits. In these circumstances the demand for intimacy becomes the demand for the public dissemination of all forms, content, and styles of intimate behavior, a demand that would negate itself by the very fact of its achievement.

Intimacy and Democratic Styles

The demand for intimacy is usually centered on immediate personal relations. But it goes beyond such relations. Since the social forms and gestures expressing intimacy convey ideas of social equality within hierarchical organizations and among professional and occupational peers, they convey acceptance or rejection by members of an elite circle. Superiors in such groups confer a sense of equality by treating others with various degrees of intimacy according to their willingness to bestow a sense of fellowship to peers. Conversely, the use of more distant and formal terms implies social, personal, political, and other forms of distance. This is true despite the fact that these social assumptions of intimacy are never as close as they are in primary social relations. Yet the sense of rejection that comes from not achieving the standard level of intimacy that implies acceptance and equality results in a desire for the democratization of the privileges of being treated equally by one's professional, occupational, political, or organizational superiors. Thus the demand for social intimacy parallels a demand for political equality, which cannot be granted so long as social, political, economic, and institutional inequalities exist. We have already noted, however, that in these areas pseudo-intimacy emerges, especially in democratic cultures that grant the appearance of intimacy to subordinates, even though the inequalities persist and the gestures of intimacy are recognized by both parties as "human relations." At times the superior "acts democratic"; he learns the first names of his subordinates; he learns the small talk that makes him human, from time to time he will confess to the human fallibilities that suggest his equality and humanity, and he metes these out in appropriate times and places. Moreover, it is likely that he will have been trained in "human relations," in leadership courses and in personality seminars, to project appearances of intimacy and humanity in nonintimate situations for the purposes of marketing himself, his personality, and/or his organization. If he (or she) is high enough in a large-scale organization, or in an organization that requires the affirmation of his personality for market or organizational success, he will have a staff of public relations experts and media merchandisers to manufacture symbols and appearances of intimacy to be carried through the impersonal networks of the mass media. As a star or celebrity, he is subject to the demands for an intimate knowledge of his personality by distant, not intimate, outsiders, and he will provide the required information by manufacturing illusions of intimacy that will meet the demand (and in some cases *create* the demand), according to his organizational, political, or marketing needs. Yet one cannot assume that the demand and the supply for illusions of intimacy or the claim and its validation are in balance. Reporters who are not always part of the bargaining network may provide intimate portrayals that damage the public credibility of those who would project managed images of the leader as intimate, as human in favorable terms. While President Nixon may have spent more time at managing his image than President Johnson or Kennedy, the portrayals of President Nixon as cheating on his income tax or grocery bills, praying with Secretary Kissinger, or attempting to keep state gifts received from the Shah of Iran violated the public relations portraits that Nixon so carefully attempted to have drawn of himself. At the same time, President Carter's campaign projection of himself as a man capable of "lust" violated other images of himself that he attempted to portray with even greater assiduousness. While it is not difficult to imagine that a virile man might have lusts for women other than his wife, the necessity to announce this to a reporter for *Playboy* magazine was not deemed appropriate by many who might have accepted such an assertion if it came from anybody but the President himself. One must assume that President-to-be Carter, in granting the interview, was managing the public image of himself as he exists at intimate levels; yet in this case it appears that he mismanaged it. Thus it appears that, for public figures, the level and content of intimate knowledge appropriate to the role is different, depending on the institution, the position, and the kind of intimacy portrayed. The level of the portrayal of intimacy permitted of a Pope is far different from that of a movie star. Knowledge of the rules which determine these levels is, at any given moment, conventionalized, though over time the rules change. Yet always there are demands for intimate knowledge, some at a personal and others at public levels, but equally there are demands for social distance, the violation of which would constitute as grave a public offense as the granting of intimacy. The preservation of privacy in public is as important as the universal demand for intimacy.

Social Class and Friendship

In all of the above, we have treated friendship, as related to the experience of success and mobility, as necessarily an aspect of interpersonal behavior, consistent with our emphasis on the emergence of special kinds and degrees of intimacy. We have focused primarily on friendship that crosses the gradient of success. Yet we have also suggested that the inevitability of different levels of success and failure is a product of pyramidal structures of opportunity due to the scarcity of success in a society that values success so highly that ultimate success is virtually unattainable. Even Presidents Eisenhower and Nixon could be overawed by the greater success of their more affluent friends. But because of the pyramidal structures of opportunity and success, most people in our society are subject to relative failure and only moderate success. In part, the judgment as to one's own relative standing is based on to whom one chooses to compare oneself and one's ability to insulate oneself from evidence that might suggest even greater failure. Even if this is true, however, most individuals objectively are not successful by the ultimate standards of success in our society, and most friendship at any time and place does not sharply cross success lines. Even so, a great part of the content of friendship takes place within the framework of social class and, as we have indicated, within class in the context of age. In the case of class, the contents of a substantial part of the friendship within the working and lower middle classes reflect the experience of *rassentiment* against those classes who project, regardless of intention, evidence of success to the outsider, especially to these classes. To the lower classes, the hypocrisy, the humiliation, the exposure of their illegitimate means, and the luck of the upper classes are a constant source of conversation. The condescension to them by the middle and upper classes is a common theme of their friendship and culture, which is catered to by some part of the mass media.

For the middle classes, the necessity to prove to oneself and one's peers the achievement of moderate success is a dominant element in friendship and cultural patterns. But this necessity also includes a necessity to avoid the evidence of even greater success by economic and social superiors and to defend one's limited success, which is so demeaned. The necessity of providing evidence of success means in fact an attitude of condescension, exclusion, tolerance, and, at best, "noblesse oblige" toward the lower classes. This last attitude may be the most insulting of all.

Finally, the upper classes, no matter how defined, can find individuals who are more successful, but they must, to celebrate their own success, condescend to individuals who, from the standpoint of their own necessities, must find evidence of their own success.

Friendship and Class Culture

We have emphasized that these defensive and aggressive gestures are largely part of the culture of classes within a society that emphasizes mobility, no matter how those classes are defined. We have also suggested that, with respect to success, there are no sharp cutting points that demarcate one social class from another. But we have also emphasized that much of what can be regarded as the culture of class is the content of friendship. But beyond this our emphasis on friendship groups that cut across success lines are evidence of both the openness of our class system and the fact that individuals have the capacity to resist the "pressure of culture" in defense of their own historical identities and the values upon which they base a substantial part of their lives. If we appear to be cynical about class cultural systems, we are less cynical about the value of friendship and intimacy as expressed in some kinds of personal behavior.*

Intimate Revelations and Intimate Concealments

One type of performance designed to conceal in public the realities of intimate behavior consists in public charades that conform, in their manifest content, to public expectations, i.e., roles, but are joint presentations to conceal their opposite.[8] To use Goffman's

---

*Of course, the dimensions of success, in any complex society, are not linear. A person who may be highly successful in business may defer to a poet, who on economic grounds is not successful or even, in the absence of better knowledge, may not be successful as a poet. At the same time, the poet may regard success in business as success, or only perhaps as a very limited form of success. The fact that the criteria of success are both multidimensional and ambiguous allows for bases of friendship across the lines of any one dimension of success and may result in a higher evaluation of the common dimensions of a friendship pair's aspirations, in whose terms neither of them has been successful. To state it differently, both friends may be successful on grounds other than those that were the basis of their friendship.

terminology, there is a total pool of dramaturgic devices in which men present the front of masculinity, with the spouse conspiring to provide the setting, the props, and the supporting character. The wife may, in a restaurant, pass the money to pay the bill under the table at the very last moment, so that the man may act the role of the beneficent provider. Observers share in the drama by looking the other way, though were the play skillfully written, the image of masculinity would have been presented without showing its artifice. The husband would have had the money in the first place. Perhaps the clumsiness in presentation is part of the play in which the wife, by making her stage management visible, enters the play and becomes the central figure, denying the performance that she, with apparent clumsiness, mars (or reveals). The audience—the others at this performance—may choose not to notice, or it may make ironical comments about the discrepancy between appearance and reality, or form and content, in which the ambiguity as to which is appearance and which is reality provides the basis for conversion of tragedy into comedy. In addition, the ironical commentary may not simply be the response of an audience but becomes part of the play, so that public roles that deny the reality of intimate behavior are, in an age of irony and skepticism, not only the source of philosophical and sociological inquiry but the object of humor, irony, and self-devaluation.

In such cases, the public roles are designed to conceal intimate behavior that is the opposite of, or at least belies the expected appropriate role behavior. The common recognition of the transparency of the roles becomes a public role in and of itself, so that we burlesque not only the public role but the intimate role. In doing so, we devalue not only the public role but the hidden behavior that the public role at one time was designed to mask. The question remains, then: Is there an intimate role or a private existence that exists beyond the masks? Certainly we have suggested that at deep psychological levels there are points where the individual becomes unaware of the sources of his behavior, and at an intimate level there are some kinds of behavior that an intimate pair or peer group may not want to acknowledge, either to each other or to outsiders. Once again, in an age of irony and skepticism, and where the tradition of self-revelation is perhaps as strong as the tradition of reserve, the habit of exposure, of confession, is so much a part of a new tradition that at times it appears to be appropriate to invent confessions, to parade the intimate, even though the intimate behavior revealed may be spurious. What may be important is only that the confession, the self-revelation be dramatic and focus attention on the self or on the need of the self to occupy for a moment the center of the stage. The norms for the public portrayal and public enactment of the private, whether true or false, have a cultural history starting perhaps with Rousseau's *Confessions,* since which an entire strand in Western literature portraying and defining humanity as the weakness, infirmity, and perversity of the private and the intimate has emerged. Certainly the emergence and the popularization of psychology, especially Freudian psychology, has led us all to "normalize" the private and intimate. But "normalization" has meant, to a large extent, the public announcement and portrayal of the intimate and the private, especially when defined as the sexual, the perverse, the weak, and the "abnormal." The normalization of the abnormal becomes part of the public role; the genuinely private, increasingly, has no place to go. Yet if this development is a vast historical change, the need for the genuinely private and intimate still persists, even though we are not always sure of the meanings and the referents of these terms. Public confession and self-revelation—at least in some settings and some situations—seem not to be inappropriate. Yet the same behavior acted out in only slightly different settings may evoke traditional responses to attempts at unwarranted intimacy. The response of silence, the changing of subjects, the expression of disapproval, the steering of a conversation away from a traditionally tabooed subject matter still exist. The sense of knowing when, even among relative strangers, the revelation of the private and intimate is tolerable or tabooed, whether it produces a sense of drama and excitement, or whether only a sense of distaste or ennui—all of these require the ability to interpret minimal cues. One can, however, ignore the cues, if in the drama of one's self-presentation one can overwhelm the opposition and produce a collective identification with the self so revealed that the initial opposition is overlooked and thus reversed. Failure in surmounting the redoubts of privacy makes the assailant appear to be a fool or to have permanently damaged himself. But, since both possibilities exist—the possibility of avoiding unwanted intimacy and that of captivating an audience by confession—and since the outcome of either strategy is problematic, one can infer that the norms in these areas are so weak that living by one's wits becomes more important than living by the norms. And this may be the only response possible in an anomic society, where the norms have become so attenuated.

Notes

1. Quoted from F. G. Bailey, *Morality and Expediency—The Folklore of Academic Politics* (Oxford: Blackwell, 1978), pp. 120-21. See also Jeremy Boissevain, *Friends of Friends: Networks, Manipulators, and Coalitions* (Oxford: Blackwell, 1974), p. 94: "Marriage, for example, means that a man must drop some relationships . . . to accommodate the influx of his wife's intimate relations. The many friendly relations a single person maintains are contingent upon his having enough time to service them and a place to meet them. Once married, a person has less opportunity to meet these persons . . . a married person has less time available."

2. "It is, in real life, normal for police and outlaws to share an interest . . . . But when they share an *identity*, when the enforcers of narcotics laws are the sellers of narcotics, when the cops are the robbers, and the investigators the coverers-up, the foundations of common truth and honesty are shattered altogether, and society requires a subtle (and lucky) combination of forces to dig itself out." Renata Adler, "Reflections on Political Scandal," *The New York Review of Books,* Dec. 8, 1977, p. 30.

3. The literature on networks is large. See Elizabeth Bott, *Family and Social Network,* 2d ed. (New York: Free Press, 1971; originally published 1957 by Tavistock, London), p. 58, *et passim*. See also C. Mitchell, ed., *Social Networks in Urban Situations* (Manchester: Manchester University Press, 1959), and his article therein, "The Concept and Use of Social Networks."

4. See Allison Davis, Burleigh B. Gardner, and Mary R. Gardner, *Deep South,* abridged ed. (Chicago, University of Chicago Press, 1956).

5. Victor Lasky: *It Didn't Start with Watergate* (New York: Dial Press, 1976).

6. Joseph Bensman and Robert Lilienfeld, "The Journalist" (chapter 12), in *Craft and Consciousness: Occupational Technique and the Development of World Images* (New York: Wiley, 1973): ". . . when the avoidance of a major scandal seems to be impossible, applied journalism will include the apparent exposure of a minor scandal in the hope that in so doing, the major scandal will be avoided . . . exposure of a specific contradiction between appearance and reality often has the effect of being an end in itself" (p. 221). Also, in relation to the exposure of scandals as a tactical device, see Adler, "Reflections on Political Scandal," pp. 30-31: "Since at least Watergate, it has been evident that in any serious scandal, to the questions Who is behind it, and Who has the most to gain, we must add another: Who wanted it known . . . the predicament is very delicate. Because we, the reporters, are suddenly in clandestine collusion with our informants. We are to that degree in each other's pockets; there is an element of corruption."

7. See the essay by Hans Speier, "The Communication of Hidden Meaning," *Social Research,* 44, No. 3 (Autumn 1977): 471-501. Speier offers a typology,

with illustrations, of many such forms of communication, among them an episode in Stendhal's *Lucien Leuwen*. The young protagonist wishes to declare his love to the Countess de Chasteller but is thwarted by the presence of a malicious gossip. He improvises a discussion, which he makes appear to be about politics in order to divert the unwelcome Miss Berard from the hidden content of the conversation. The Countess de Chasteller, by taking up the masked style of speaking, signals to Lucien her complicity. "The listeners who do not understand covert meanings are often felt to be ludicrous, since they suffer from a defect: like some dull-witted censors, they fail to comprehend what is going on, and dupes are comical characters par excellence" (pp. 480–82).

8. Much of Erving Goffman's work is central to this discussion. See especially *The Presentation of Self in Everyday Life* (Garden City, N.Y.: Anchor Books, 1959), Chapter VI, "The Arts of Impression Management" *et passim*.

Chapter 7

The Political Dimensions of the Public and the Private

The concepts of *public* and *private* are central to sociology, anthropology, social psychology—all the human sciences; they are also central to political theory. Some implications of the conception of the public and the private will be explored here.

The public and the private can be conceived of as ways of classifying social roles, the social expectancies and the private exemptions from expectancies placed upon the behavior of individuals in specified social and political situations. These roles define, among other things, the appropriate behavior of citizens as political participants. Roles are also means for transforming generalized moralities into specific behavioral models. As such, they embody both existing states of public opinion and the past and latent norms that may underlie public opinion.

But public roles are always more than the embodiment of political codes and moralities. They are codes for acting in a wide variety of public and social situations. They include ceremonial, religious, economic, recreational, and, in fact, all social behavior subject to social definition.[1]

Privacy, in the light of the above, includes the delimitation of some behavior as being reserved—within prescribed limits—solely for individual discretion. Thus, privacy and private behavior are defined socially.

All definitions of the social and the private are the product of historical, social, political, and cultural development and articulation, and cannot be said to exist *sui generis;* they can emerge from the very biological, physiological, and psychological character of the human species, but they have emerged, as we have seen, as the result of long but steady processes of historical, social, ideological, cultural, and economic development.

A principal contention of this chapter is that the conception of the "public" and the "private" is, in addition, at any historical moment a set of analytical polarities and legal distinctions presenting logical problems that are not easily resolvable. "Public" and "private" are not fixed states or territorial realms that have concrete, fixed properties.

In primitive and ancient societies the distinction between the public and private does not exist. The individual, linguistically and intellectually, is so deeply integrated into an extended family system and into locality-based social relationships—usually defined by tradition—that all of his or her behavior (and that of all others) is subject to mutual surveillance, so much so that the individual cannot conceive of himself as having an identity apart from the family, tribe, or neighborhood. Conceptions of separate private and public "domains" are minimal. To the extent that "individuals" attempt to withdraw from the group, they are often thought of as practicing witchcraft and sorcery.

The foundations for conceptions of the private, as a separate sphere of consciousness and activity, emerge when individuals are able to separate themselves from the locality, the family, and the omnipresence and omnipotence of the tribe. Social distance makes privacy possible, and this distance is politically the result of the expropriation of kinship property by tribal and kinship leaders. It is also the result of the attempt of others to create a social base for limiting the exploitation and oppression of emerging kings and princes. At an intellectual level, conceptions of privacy emerge out of the attempt to justify the unequal distribution (among individuals) of good and bad fortune.

The conception of the public as an ideal, embodied in civic virtue, public morality, and citizenship, thus emerges in response to the growth of a sphere of private autonomy. In the attempt to work out new civic moralities, the public duties of the citizen to an abstract polis or state were defined. But the citizen then is defined as a separate individual, freed from submergence in the kin group, the tribe, and the locality. The reforms of Solon, Kleisthenes particularly, and Pisistratus are crucial in this regard. These experiments in the definition of the public and private were repeated in Rome and in medieval cities up until the rise of the modern state. They still persist when new populations achieve political consciousness and enter the arena of political participation.

Historically both the public and the private emerge as opposite faces of the same coin, both in opposition to traditional roles that entail no such opposition. Given this early historical unity of what later became the public and the private and their later empirical separation, the attempt to resolve the contradictions between the public and the private simply by denying their opposition or suggesting at normative levels that the opposition ought not exist denies the empirical (and, as we shall see, the logical) problems involved in this opposition.

The opposition of the public and the private is a result of the dissolution of primitive and ancient traditional roles and results in another set of polarities. The same person is both the actor of public roles and the legatee of private rights (in various combinations and mixtures, in different times and places). It is necessary to avoid reifying or personifying the public and the private as separate entities and seeing them as battling over the individual, or seeing the private as individuals battling the state. The state—that is, governments and regimes—is made up of individuals who have a separate private existence, while on the other hand no individual can be abstracted from the social and public networks that are subject to social and political definition.

Despite the assertion that conceptions of the public and the private are historically emerging definitions, it is possible—perhaps as social definition—to conceive of the private—as we have done—as a biological, physiological, and psychological category, upon which social definitions are overlaid.

We have conceived of the private as partially based on the uniqueness of the experience of pain. Sympathy and empathy are social, based upon the recall of one's own pain in response to the external manifestations of pain in another. But pain as felt in its original experience cannot be shared except as transformed by sympathy and empathy.[2] The private can be conceived of as unsocialized drives, needs, and "instincts," some of which are below the level of the individual's consciousness. Privacy can be a constituent of neurosis and psychosis—as in the extreme case of catatonia.[3] Insanity can be, and has been, defined as the extreme inability to project and receive undistorted communication, an involuntary privacy that often includes separation from oneself.

Finally, privacy includes means of protection of the self from overburdening pressures of public roles. Every acceptance of a public role entails the repression, channelizing, and deflection of "private" or personal attention, motives, and demands upon the self in order to address oneself to the expectations of others. Minimally this means directing one's attention outward. It means accepting objective, external social and technological procedures. It includes deferral, postponement, and repression of private motives that are inappropriate, not grantable, or negatively sanctioned according to the social and public norms that govern a role situation and are internalized by the other parties to that situation. Acceptance of public roles means the withholding or concealment of private thoughts and actions that violate public norms. Violations are considered deviant, criminal, "antisocial," unconventional, or stigmatized. Such behavior must be transformed into publicly and socially acceptable terms and appearances.

Within each individual, then, public and social roles, private motives, and self-definition are present, and they are often in conflict. The existence of social and public roles, norms, and codes means a denial of some aspect of the antisocial, presocial motives and impulses of the individual and a channelization of biologically based impulses into socially accepted patterns of action. Even when "society" defines socially acceptable objects and goals of action and the publically acceptable means to such action, as Merton has illustrated, it does not consistently link the socially defined means to the socially approved goals.[4] The means may not be available, or else, to add to Merton's analysis, when the means become available, goals are escalated. As a result private motives are often out of phase with public goals.

One, and only one, of the many possibilities that exist in this situation is that individuals may link themselves into social relationships, groups, and networks, which give recognition to the needs, desires, and interests whose expression are not publicly permitted, or whose public expression is deemed inappropriate. At one extreme the criminal association is an informally organized alternative group structure, separate from legally sanctioned associations. Similarly the netherworld of the stigmatized and perverted may become socially organized to provide an area for acting out one's private motives and gaining social acceptance within a social circle. But far more important for consideration of the concept of the private are those types of less deviant social structures which permit the expression of personal sentiments and the performance of actions that are not publicly sanctioned or are officially proscribed. These "informal" or intimate social relations include within their ambience the confession of socially interdicted actions; the overcoming of guilt induced by deviating from public norms; the gaining at intimate and informal levels of social support against the prospect of social isolation; collective participation in officially proscribed actions; and the achievement of love, affection, and recognition of one's own uniqueness despite the violation of official norms.[5] These may include, of course, simple social exchanges that are not specified in public or official codes or formal codes of etiquette. They also include the simple enjoyment of sociability and the pursuit of values that are neither stigmatized nor officially sanctioned.

Social groups and networks that achieve some of these functions are criminal and deviant groups, recreational and civil groups within country clubs, whose members, restricted in number, are allowed to express deviant aspects of their behavior that they are not allowed to express in more public situations. Friendship, colleagueship, the family, and love relationships are, of course, social relations whose very existence rests on the suspension of official and public role demands in favor of the recognition of the unique individual as he or she is or believes himself/herself to be.*

These informal social groups and networks can be called the *intimate.* They permit social expression of the *private,* but because they are social expressions they are not private. They are, as we have seen, the threshold of the quasi-public, having some characteristics of the private and some of the public. They allow the expression of sentiments and attitudes that are denied by official, public morality but allow them in social relations that are less than open, public situations.

They too have their own rules. Ideally, they should be symmetrical; that is, one ought not reveal more to the other than the other

---

*The confidentiality of the confession, the legal immunities from public revelation of the medical doctor or attorney (and the hoped for but not achieved confidentiality of a reporter's sources) are legitimated equivalents of this kind of privacy. So too is the immunity of the individual from the requirements of testifying against a spouse or himself.

reveals to oneself. They ought not to be exploitative; they should be based on love, trust, and deep affection. These role relations should not be narrow, segmental, and rational. If they are, they fail to satisfy those needs that are peculiarly rewarded in intimate relations. They include exchanges of favors, privileges, and opportunities that are denied in public codes. These favors may be "graft," corruption, nepotism, "influence," and all the illegal "perks" of office. But the "rules" of intimate social relations entail restraints. They include being willing to maintain the secrets that are communicated in intimate social relationships, if not totally, then confining divulgence to others who are part of the interlocking network of personal trust.[6] This sense of trust includes a norm of "not squealing" to public authorities or not allowing informal communications to enter public and official media of communications.

Thus the quasi-public includes reports of actions and sentiments that violate public norms, but only in quasi-public networks that may parallel public networks.

The quasi-public is broader than the intimate, just as the intimate includes more than dyadic relationships, i.e., mutually oriented social relationships that are so bounded as to preclude third parties. Each party to a dyadic relationship may be party to other intimate relationships. He or she is likely to be a friend or colleague and related to more than the other party in the dyad. Thus both the witnessing and the communication that are part of the dyad are reported to third parties, who, as intimate others, may further communicate the reports of deviant behavior and thought. The network of informal communication may be as long as the interlocking chains of intimacy. As the information so reported (sometimes labeled gossip, rumor, or inside dope) is communicated at distant linkages from the original witnesses or actors, it becomes watered down, distorted, perhaps overdramatized, and regarded as inaccurate or unverifiable. Yet much of the information originally witnessed and communicated and reported in an extended network is precisely the same information that is regarded as private or intimate knowledge. Much of that information is reports of deviant, illegal, scandalous, or disesteemed behavior that violates the public norms, public codes, and public role expectations. Moreover, much of intimate social relationships and their extensions through interlocking networks arise in the feeling that public roles, norms, and codes are too severe, demanding, and restrictive to serve the private needs and motives of the participants in the network.

Thus there are three "realms" of public and private morality: the private, the public, and the quasi-public. Quasi-publics have their own norms, rules, and moralities, different from and opposed to the official norms of the law and the publicly celebrated norms of public, civic, and communal moralities even when these are not embodied in the law. But the quasi-public differs from the private in that it allows social expression of sentiments and behavior that are denied by public morality.

To conceive of these areas of behavior—the public, the private, and quasi-public—as separate and distinct realms falsifies the problem. The three realms, to repeat, are analytical distinctions, referring to aspects of behavior that are practiced by the same individual. Thus every official or every individual who acts in public exists as a private individual. At some times, like Javert in *Les Miserables,* he may attempt to deny his existence as a private individual, and at all times —like Caesar's wife—he is supposed to be beyond criticism. Yet he remains, in some aspects of his self, a private person. And most individuals have networks of interpersonal relationships, intimate relationships that interlace and interweave around their public roles.

For the same reason, a pluralistic conception that private and public roles embrace totally different social realms is a reification. One can think of "the family," the peer group, and the clique, as well as "the state" or civic associations, as each being an enclosed social realm, each representing a special locus of particularization or universalism. Friendship networks and colleague networks, as we have suggested, surround, interlace, and intertwine with formal organizations, but the "boundaries" of informal networks are not identical with those of formal organizations. Informal networks may interlace with only one segment of a governmental or other formal organization, and they may extend across a wide variety of both formal and informal organizations, including various family and network structures. The distinctions between public and private, informal and formal are legal and administrative distinctions governing selected aspects of completely interwoven behavior. They are expectations that can be made of the same individuals in roughly the same time and space. They are not separations in the topography of actions, not entities that face each other in personified opposition.

This distinction is important in the following way. The "state" in action must be conceived as the actions of individuals in response to selected official roles. The "state" is composed of individuals, and those individuals are members of intimate circles and the social networks that at some levels violate public and civic morality.[7] Since such violations reflect deep human and biological needs of individuals, both those needs and the informal codes of quasi-public moralities are always and inevitably present in the "state." Despite insistence on public morality in the exercise of public and official roles, the individuals who occupy public or official positions are constrained by their very existence to violate it. Officials abuse power, profit from their social position, and engage in illegalities and violation of law and public morality. If they do not and are unusually scrupulous, they can hardly avoid being witness to such violations. If they are not witnesses, they are recipients of reports of violations. As officials they are obligated to report such violations to superiors and law enforcement officials, who themselves may be members of informal networks and are thus pulled in contradictory directions by their private interests and motives, their network loyalties, and the obligation of their official roles and of a more general public morality. If they are exclusively responsive to public moralities, they may be excluded from informal networks that make a personal and private life possible—that is, they are adjudged informers, righteous prigs, and cold, impersonal, inhuman bureaucrats. In addition, they may cut themselves off from those informal networks that make possible the realization of private interests through the exercise of their public position. Finally, if they were to insist on the reporting and prosecution of *all* illegalities and misuse of official position, they might have little time to fulfill their manifest public roles or achieve positive action. Some degree of tolerance, benign neglect, and overlooking of deviancy is necessary to remain human, sentient individuals working in legal and administrative frameworks that are primarily defined by public or official roles and moralities. The question remains, given these structures: What are the boundaries between public, private, and quasi-public roles and codes.

For the moment, we can conclude that state, government, or public and social institutions cannot be deemed the ultimate repository of public moralities. State, government, and formal organizations are necessarily flawed with the humanity of private weaknesses and quasi-public moralities. Thus the righteous individual may report a major crime, misues of power, or dereliction of duty to the official with jurisdiction, not knowing that the official in question is the instigator of the crime or a deeply committed member of the informal network that embraces the crime.[8] The master criminal may be the Attorney General of the United States or even the President.

He may be minister of police, as was Balzac's Vautrin, a literary notion once regarded as totally improbable. The criminal network may include congressmen investigating the receipt of bribes by other congressmen and perhaps by themselves. Or the law enforcement agency may be part of the entire elite structure of a socialist or democratic society that itself systematically violates public morality or its ideology of equality of rewards and of opportunity.

Yet, while we speak of the flawed state as an ever present empirical possibility—and too often a reality—we cannot as a matter of course think of the free, rational, heroic individual, the citizen, as the repository of public morality. All our characterization of privacy, intimacy, and the constraints of membership in quasi-public networks apply to the private citizen even more than they do to officials.

Whether as citizens or as officials in governmental or nongovernmental organizations, we are all constrained by our existence as private individuals, as intimates and as members of quasi-public networks, to be tolerant of violations of public moralities or to be violators ourselves. On the other hand, all but the total psychopath realize that excessive or extreme violations of public morality and legality make social life impossible, and this realization by the individual living in society is the ultimate basis of the social contract. If the pursuit of private interests and network conspiracy is unlimited but decentralized, it is the war of each against all. If violations of public moralities by an elite network are carried on through the use of state machinery, then the state becomes a means of war against the many by the few. In such cases cynicism among the many is the response to violations of public morality by the organized official violators. Then the state machinery and, in fact, all public institutions become the object of distrust; counter-criminality, illegality, and violations of public morality become a quasi-public alternative to trust in and use of public institutions as means for carrying out ordinary, everyday action.

The realization of the necessity to maintain limits on violation of the norms of public morality goes hand in hand with the necessity of maintaining private interests and intimate and quasi-public roles and codes. Given these contradictions, the basic questions remains: How are these boundaries between the private, public, and quasi-public defined? Where are the mechanisms of such definition? When and how are they invoked? What are the conditions for the operations of such mechanisms? And how are "adequate" boundaries maintained, assuming that the criterion of adequacy becomes socially available?

Some obvious answers suggest themselves immediately.

First, individuals with private grievances, personal pique, spite, or desire for vengeance may "blow the whistle" on crime, the violation of legal codes, or more generalized violations of public morality. Regardless of whether or not the report of the violation is caused by personal spite or genuine moral indignation, the report of violation in the public media, its transfer from intimate or quasi-public networks of communication to public and official networks, constitutes a challenge to appropriate official bodies to respond. Reports in quasi-public channels of networks can be ignored or dismissed; they are only "rumors and gossip." Once those reports enter public and official channels, the appropriate law-enforcement agents (even those involved in the informal illegitimate networks) have to take action if such reports persist. If they do not take action the officials may risk public censure for violation of their official roles.

Second, private interests and ambitions become transformed into issues of public morality when the ambitious prosecutor, legislator, or candidate investigates or otherwise makes a political issue of law violation or the public immorality of those in power. Again the private motives of the whistle-blower are less important than the consequences of bringing the private or quasi-public violations of public roles, codes, or law and immorality into public, official view and of destroying the ability of others to perform intimate and quasi-public roles and obligations that are in violation of official or public roles.

Third, the press and media of mass communications can, as investigatory journalists, as muckrakers, and as gossipers, raise the violations of public morality to a public issue. The process of transforming private, intimate, and quasi-public violations of public morality into public issues and of documenting the violations can be undertaken regardless of whether the media select for themselves the role of tribune of the people or conceive of the report of dramatic violations of public moralities as merely an exercise of professionalism or as a means to sell time and space. It can take place even when the press and the reporter are violators of public morality in other aspects of their operation.[9]

Finally, a sincere sense of outrage on the part of a citizen for some violations of public codes may cause public reporting even when the citizen may be the violator of other moral codes whose violation he regards as less offensive than the ones he reports.

The process of creating the moral issues that define public morality rests ultimately on the capacity of a public to be outraged. That is, reports of such violations may be absorbed without producing moral indignation because of existing cynicism, tolerance, or overfamiliarity with a tradition of public immorality. The reports may be too abstract or distant to provide comprehension or a basis for emotional identification with the victims. They may not provide sufficient concrete evidence or detail, that is, there may be no "smoking gun," to allow for the separation of the report from "mere rumor or gossip." Journalistic or other publicity at official and public levels with respect to even a single dramatic violation of public morality must be continuous and sustained if it is to overcome the blase attitude of the public.

This too invites problems. Inaccurate, undramatic, undocumented, and random charges of public immorality invite greater public cynicism and apathy, making the achievement of a sense of outrage more difficult in the future. The very procedures and processes that generate the effective operation of public morality when badly done negate that very operation when well done.

A final note must be added. It is difficult to define the content of operative public morality in the abstract or to conceive of it as an entity. If the boundaries of public morality were, at any one moment, clearly defined and well known, and the detection and reporting predictable, each potential violator could stay a hair's breadth within those boundaries; quasi-public and private deviancy could be contained by public morality. There would thus be no conflict—that is, ambiguity— between "the public" and the "private."

Fortunately or unfortunately, the sources of outrage are not predictable. Thus the malefactor may attempt to "stonewall" it and succeed. The official who is a violator may successfully attempt to avoid enforcement against the crimes in whose performance he is a quasi-public conspirator. Stonewalling, delay, and inaction are all based upon predictions of the responsiveness of public opinion to the manipulation of a yet to be crystallized public opinion, whether or not that manipulation is done by the exposers or the exposed. The accuracy of those predictions are tested only by the amount of *ex post facto* outcry. Thus public morality is not an entity. It is shapeless and undefined, a potential response to specific issues. The actual, operative definitions are made by the response to specific exposures, including their prosecution. Each exposure and prosecution, and the attendant public issues and outcry, define for the moment only the existing state of public morality and the particular public norms that are made salient by that exposure.[10]

It is the continuity of exposure, outcry, and prosecution over and through time that constitutes the significant means of discerning operative public morality. In the periods between such exposures, the normality of the private, the intimate, and the quasi-public constitutes an ever continuous normalization and humanization of public codes or morality. In those periods of "normality" it is the memory of past and the prospect of future exposures and enforcement that guarantee the effectiveness of public morality as a constraint on private and quasi-public interests and deviancy.

Summary and Conclusions

We have suggested that the private and public are inextricably intertwined and interlaced. They cannot be treated as separate entities. The private and the intimate have many psychological and social functions, one of which is the individual's reaction to and protection from the demands of what are felt to be both the necessary and the too severe demands of public morality.

The private is in necessary conflict with the public, but public morality at some levels is felt by almost everyone to be necessary to both private and social survival.

The individual is flawed by his private biological and personal needs and motives. The state, government, or regime is flawed by the fact that officials who are the guarantors of public morality are, among other things, private individuals.

A normal "compromise" between private needs and public institutions and social needs is the social network that creates quasi-public cultures, which are less demanding than public moralities and whose own norms violate public codes while humanizing social and private life.

While quasi-public networks have their own particular moral systems, the operation of these systems may violate internalized public moralities of some of its members and may produce private resentments, grievances, and spite. The violations may be used, additionally, as an opportunity to achieve "rationally expedient" private motives by invoking public morality as a check upon private and quasi-public behavior that violates public morality. Public morality is ultimately defined by outrage at the violation of latent public codes.

The necessary conditions for such mechanisms of definition of public morality are:

1. Freedom of the press (subject to minimal libel and slander laws), and with it minimal freedom of press from a "corruption" which necessarily occurs. Included in "freedom of the press" are the persistence and nerve of investigative reporters.

2. The possibility of ultimate recourse to popular political controls, which make officials responsive to outrage public morality when moral indignation is invoked by exposure. The existence of some levels of democracy and public representation is a minimal precondition for public morality among those groups that hold themselves or are held accountable to public morality. Without democracy or popular representation, there is no opportunity to limit the operation of the quasi-public illegalities of officials. This is not to say that democratic regimes are intrinsically moral. We can only say that democratic and representative regimes provide the opportunity to "throw the rascals out," even if the rascals are only going to be replaced by another crew of rascals. Undemocratic regimes institutionalize illegalities and convert crime into legality, or at least they use legalist formulae. They also, as we have indicated, make necessary the development of counter-crime and the distrust of the machinery of the state.

3. At some level, the above necessary conditions can be effective only when there is a deep and long-term political socialization to political morality.

4. To be effective, political socialization must be confirmed by a minimal prosecution of violations of existing standards. Otherwise the existence of institutionalized quasi-public crime, especially at elite or privileged levels, produces cynicism, apathy, distrust of public institutions, and counter-crime, with a level of public morality so low that "the state" can be held together only by force and cynical expediency at marginal levels of societal efficiency.

This argument is in some sense circular: Public immorality breeds public immorality; and reasonable law enforcement breeds acceptance of public morality. Yet the crucial variable is the possibility that those who in some sense accept the necessity of public morality despite their private interests can make public institutions and officials responsive to the minimal demands of existing public moral standards.

The precise content and the substantive levels of public morality are continuously subject to revision in any time and place. Charismatic movements, moral crusades, religious and civic movements, and revivals may contribute to the definition and redefinition of the prevailing and emerging content of public morality. Such movements usually occur in response to crises in public morality, following deep disillusionment with or breakdowns of established standards of public morality and order.

The existence of freedom to expose and enforce public morality is, of course, only one factor in the definition of the current levels of public morality, as is the continuous erosion of public morality by the particularism of the private, the intimate, and the quasi-public. But no stable equilibrium between these two factors has so far ever been achieved over any length of time. New levels and new content are continually asserted and reasserted in the face of continuous erosions of older levels.

Economic and political innovation and development alter existing equilibriums. When these accumulate, sharp and decisive breaks in public morality are likely to occur, requiring specific historical explanations relative to their time, place, and the innovations in questions. Yet, as we have speculated, the specific *processes* are always similar.

Notes

1. For a history of changing definitions of appropriate and inappropriate social behavior, see Norbert Elias, *The Civilizing Process: The History of Manners,* trans. Edmund Jephcott (New York: Urizen Books, 1978). The German-language edition was published in 1939.

2. See above, chapter 3, pp. 54–57.

3. See above, chapter 3, pp. 67–69.

4. Robert Merton, *Social Theory and Social Structure,* 1957 ed., Chapter V, "Continuities in the Theory of Social Structure and Anomie."

5. For one such study, see David Gadd, *The Loving Friends: A Portrait of Bloomsbury* (New York, Harcourt Brace Jovanovich, 1974).

6. See above, chapter 6, pp. 153–55.

7. Joseph Bensman and Bernard Rosenberg, "Politics and Society" (chapter 15), in *Mass, Class and Bureaucracy: An Introduction to Sociology* (New York: Praeger, 1976), pp. 427–66, esp. pp. 463–66.

8. See Renata Adler, "Reflections on Political Scandal," *New York Review of Books,* Dec. 8, 1977, p. 30.

9. See above, p. 178.

10. See Hans Speier, "The Historical Development of Public Opinion," originally published in the *American Journal of Sociology,* January 1950, and reprinted as chapter 24 of Speier, *Social Order and the Risks of War: Papers in Political Sociology,* repring (Cambridge, Mass.: MIT Press, 1969), pp. 323–38. On p. 336: "The expectation that public opinion safeguards morality and promotes reasonableness in foreign policy was nowhere entertained with greater optimism than in the United States." *Sic transit gloria mundi.*

Indexes

Index of Names

Index of Subjects

alienation, 67
ancient society, 38, 41, 172
  role configurations in, viii
anticipatory socialization, 6
axial age of history, 29

capitalism, 47–48
Catholicism
  confession in, 161
  monastic, 43
character disorder, 58–59
charisma, 37
Christianity, early, 38
cities and public roles, 39–43
citizenship, 41–42
civic roles, morality, virtue, 41–43,
  172
class structure
  and deviants, 62–63
  and friendship, 165–166
  and media exposure, 34–35
  and privacy, 30–32
  and public appearances, 33–34
  and roles, 18–21, 41–43

confession
  as part of friendship, 158-161
  as psychotherapy, 62–63, 161
confidentiality, 175
conformity, 4, 6
corporations, providing role models,
  4–5
counter-culture within groups and organizations, 76
cultural values as a source of conflict,
  91–92

dehumanization as repression of self,
  23
democracy and intimacy, 163–164
deviancy, deviants, 7-8, 49, 58–66, 76,
  77–78, 80, 93, 157, 168, 177–178
  normal deviancy, 63–66
  tolerance among deviants, 61

economics, economic individualism,
  44–50
ego ideal, 2
ethical standards, 3–4

193